THE ART OF
JUDGMENT

THE ART OF JUDGMENT

10 Steps to Becoming a More Effective Decision-Maker

JOHN ADAIR

BLOOMSBURY BUSINESS
LONDON · OXFORD · NEW YORK · NEW DELHI · SYDNEY

BLOOMSBURY BUSINESS
Bloomsbury Publishing Plc
50 Bedford Square, London, WC1B 3DP, UK

BLOOMSBURY, BLOOMSBURY BUSINESS and the Diana logo are
trademarks of Bloomsbury Publishing Plc

First published in Great Britain 2020

A catalogue record for this book is available from the British Library

Library of Congress Cataloguing-in-Publication data has been applied for

ISBN: 978-1-4729-8070-0; eBook: 978-1-4729-8071-7

2 4 6 8 10 9 7 5 3 1

Typeset by Deanta Global Publishing Services, Chennai, India
Printed and bound in Great Britain by CPI Group (UK) Ltd, Croydon CR0 4YY

To find out more about our authors and books visit www.bloomsbury.com
and sign up for our newsletters

CONTENTS

CONTENTS

Introduction

*What then is Time? If nobody asks me I know; but if
I wanted to explain it to someone that should ask me,
plainly I do not know.*

ST AUGUSTINE

MUCH THE SAME could be said about judgment. 'Looking back, I acted against my better judgment in marrying him,' a friend who has recently separated from her husband remarked to me yesterday. Like most people, I knew well enough what she meant by 'judgment'. But ask me to explain it – let alone teach it – and I struggle. Nor am I alone in this respect. Which may account for the fact that previous attempts to write a book on the art of judgment can be numbered on the fingers of one hand.

Yet great importance is commonly attributed to the quality of having good judgment in a person, and especially in a leader. 'Reason and calm judgment, the qualities especially belonging to a leader,' wrote the Roman historian Tacitus.

In one very large opinion poll before an American presidential election, three-quarters of the voters of all parties rated 'sound judgment' the top desirable quality, ranking it as more important than high ethical standards, compassion, frankness, experience, willingness to compromise and party loyalty.[1] But in the run-up to elections anywhere in the world, this key quality is seldom addressed, perhaps not least because of the difficulty in defining it.

The way ahead

Achieving a dictionary-like definition of judgment is far less important than forming a clear idea of the concept. Therefore, Part One of this book is devoted to understanding judgment as a process – a universal one – through which we take our minds when, looking ahead, we experience real difficulty in deciding which way to go.

It is perhaps possible for academics to sit on the fence forever about many questions, endlessly debating the possible answers, but leadership exists in the world of time and chance: it is about

---

[1] Quoted in Renshon, Stanley A. 'Appraising Good Judgment Before It Matters' in *Good Judgment in Foreign Policy: Theory and Application*, Renshon, Stanley A. and Larson, Deborah Welch eds. New York: Rowman & Littlefield, 2003.

action. That reality is the theme of Part Two. Amid conditions of uncertainty, complexity and turbulence, how can leaders both make the right decisions and take their people with them on the journey?

Each chapter focuses on a subject highly relevant to the art of judgment and does so in a practical way. For the purpose of this book is to give you opportunities – ten of them in all – to improve your own powers of judgment. It is worth remembering, too, that the best judges are generally those who are aware how much human beings – including themselves – are predisposed to misjudgment.

How to use this book

In order to stimulate your thinking beyond the compass of these ten chapters, at the end of each one I summarize the discussion in some simple key points. These are not merely summaries, however, for sometimes new thoughts are born in them.

Some checklists are also included. Again, they are not of the rather mundane type that serve to remind you if you have packed everything before going on holiday. They are designed to help you to relate the ideas of this book to your own situation: your particular needs, problems and opportunities. For we learn only when the sparks jump to and fro between ideas and experience, theory and practice:

PRINCIPLES   ⟶   EXPERIENCE

or   and   or

THEORY   ⟵   PRACTICE

As it is when connections occur between these two poles – the general and the actual – that learning occurs, you need both. The various case studies and examples in this book are designed to be 'stepping stones' to that end:

PRINCIPLES ⟶ THIRD-PERSON ⟶ YOUR

EXAMPLES   EXPERIENCE

Equally, the process must work in reverse. Your practical knowledge, gleaned from both observation of actual leaders and your own practical experience, must be brought to bear in a constructively critical way on the ideas presented in this book. The more time and thought you invest in reflecting on these key points and in answering these checklists, the more fruitful you will find the exercise. And so it takes both experience and reflection to make meaningful progress in the art of judgment. The journey is a long one – lifelong, in fact – so I can only guide you for part of the way and bring you to the point where you can face with confidence the judgment calls that lie ahead in the adventure that is your life. Then, as Marcel Proust in effect says, it will be all up to you:

> *We do not receive wisdom; we must discover it for ourselves after a journey that no one can take for us or spare us.*

PART ONE

UNDERSTANDING JUDGMENT

1

Thinking to some purpose

Thought is not a trick, or an exercise, or a set of dodges,
Thought is a man in his wholeness wholly attending.

D.H. LAWRENCE

WE EXPERIENCE THINKING as a kind of a holistic activity. It is something our minds seem to do as if of their own accord, whether we like it or not, and it can take many different shapes or forms. Who hasn't spent some idle moment daydreaming of this or that? At other times, however, our holistic mind is in harness: you are thinking to some purpose.

Incidentally, the word *holistic* (from the Greek *holos*, whole) entered the English dictionary in 1926, coming from a book published that year entitled *Holism and Evolution*. Jan Christian Smuts (1870–1950), the South African statesman and soldier, was its author. During his youthful post-graduate studies in plant biology at Cambridge University, Smuts had conceived a 'big idea'. It concerned the way in which nature works, especially in the context of living organisms such as plants and humans: 'This whole-making or holistic tendency,' he wrote, 'is fundamental in nature.' There you have it in one sentence. Furthermore, he argued, the human mind is a living organism and it therefore works holistically when addressing a purpose of one kind or another.

SMUTS ON THINKING TO SOME PURPOSE

THE MOST SIGNIFICANT ELEMENT, however, in the 'field' of Mind concerns the future, and makes the future an operative factor in the present mental activity. Mind does this through purpose; purpose is the function of Mind by which it contemplates some future desired end and makes the idea of this end exert its full force in the present.

Thus I form a purpose to go on a hunting expedition for my next holiday, and this purpose forms a complex synthesis and sets going a whole series of plans and actions all intended to give effect to the purpose. Thus in purpose the future as an object in my mind becomes operative in the present and sets going and controls a long train of acts leading up to the execution of the purpose. The conscious purpose, the end as deliberately envisaged and intended, falls, of course, within the conscious inner area of Mind; but numerous subsidiary elements in the plan would operate subconsciously.

It will be noticed that purpose or purposive activity involves much more than merely the influence of the future on the present. Purpose is the most complete proof of the freedom and creative power of the mind in respect of its material and other conditions, of its power to create its own conditions and to bring about its own situations for its own free activities.

My purposive action is action which I have myself planned, which is not impressed on me or dictated to me by external necessity, and for the performance of which I take my own self-chosen measures. Through purpose the mind becomes at last master in its own house, with the power to carry out its own wishes and shape its own course, uninfluenced by the conditions of the environment.

Again, purposive activity is peculiarly holistic. Elements both of the actual past and of anticipated future experience are fused with the present experience into one individual act, which as a conscious object of the mind dominates the entire situation within the purview of the purpose or plan. It involves not only sensations and perceptions, but also concepts of a complex character, feelings and desires in respect of the end desired, and volitions in respect of the act intended; and all these elements are fused and blended into one unique purpose, which is then put into action or execution. Purpose is thus probably the highest, most complex manifestation of the free, creative, holistic activity of Mind.

Back safely on our own planet, the British astronaut Tim Peake also emphasized the supreme importance of having purposes in our lives; above all, they give us a sense of meaning, he said. He was speaking in Peterborough Cathedral in 2018 to accompany the Tim Peake's Spacecraft exhibition, which displayed the Soyuz capsule that had brought him back safe and sound from the International Space Station in 2016. From it, Peake said, that famous distant view of the blue planet Earth – our home in space – had inspired in him a sense of wonder and a profound change of perspective on life. Not, he added, faith in the religious sense. However, he went on to say that his mind remained open to the idea that the universe may be the result of intelligent design.

'What I do think is important,' Peake continued, 'is *whether we feel we have a purpose*. It doesn't matter whether one believes in God or not; what matters is having a sense of purpose... our sense of purpose should be about how we lead our lives and our relationship with others. That's what I believe in.'

It is because we are born for purpose that we are born to think.

Purposive thinking

But what actually happens when we do think in a deliberative way? It isn't easy to find out by introspection, for the simple reason our minds cannot do two things at once. As C.S. Lewis pointed out:

> You cannot hope and also think about hoping at the same moment; for in hope we look to hope's object and we interrupt this by (so to speak) turning round to look at the hope itself.

Of course the two activities can and do alternate with great rapidity; but they are distinct and incompatible... But if so, it followed that all introspection is in one respect misleading. In introspection we try to look 'inside ourselves' and see what is going on. But nearly everything that was going on a moment before is stopped by the very act of our turning to look at it...

It is as if we know the two bookends of thinking but struggle to understand what comes in between them. For, as the American philosopher John Dewey writes in *How We Think* (2007 edition):

The two limits of every unit of thinking are a perplexed, troubled, or confused situation at the beginning, and a cleared up, unified, resolved situation at the close.

In a much-reprinted early book, *Clear Thinking* (1936), R.W. Jepson – a retired headteacher – provides us with what might be called a generic bridge between these two end points. It is a span resting on six arches:

Stage 1. **Interest**: *the thinker becomes aware of the problem and their interest is aroused.*

Stage 2. **Attention**: *the problem is formulated and the relevant data collected and examined.*

Stage 3. **Suggestion**: *possible solutions occur.*

Stage 4.   **Reasoning**: *the consequences of each suggested solution are worked out.*

Stage 5.   **Conclusion**: *the most satisfactory solution is adopted.*

Stage 6.   **Test**: *the adopted suggestion is submitted to trial.*

1. Interest

In Stage 1, the thinker's interest is aroused and comes fully alive; and that is an indispensable preliminary to all purposive thinking. Mere curiosity is not enough to stimulate constructive thought. For example, you may hear a strange sound which causes you a momentary curiosity, but your interest remains dormant. You may dismiss the occurrence from your mind as being of no consequence to you. In these circumstances no thinking follows, for it is only when interest ignites that sustained thinking occurs: interest is the fuel of the mind.

2. Attention

In Stage 2, the first step the thinker takes is to *analyse* the situation – to break it up into its constituent elements in order to separate those that do and those that do not present any difficulty. The various facts and conditions bearing upon the problem are collected, verified, sorted, arranged and examined, and their significance – singly or in groups – assessed in the light of previous judgments. Then the thinker proceeds as it were to crystallize the problem and to put it into words in the form of a question or, in the case of a complicated problem, of a series of questions.

So always ask yourself what is the exact point at issue. Try to put the fundamental question in as simple and definite terms as possible and to strip it of all other questions that are of secondary importance or merely confuse the issue. For it is essential to the success of the whole operation that the questions you are addressing should be framed as clearly, as definitely, and as precisely as possible.

Indeed, in many problems this may be the crucial stage for very often when we have got down to the heart of the problem and propounded the fundamental question which is causing perplexity, the solution will be reached without much difficulty. It is as if finding and defining the right question is 50 per cent of the solution, the key to the door. By contrast, asking yourself vague indeterminate questions will often get you nowhere.

Complex questions should therefore be avoided where possible. Again, in some problematic situations, the question may be framed for us and here it is essential that we should spend a little time pondering over the terms carefully and finding out exactly what is required.

When the preliminary ground has been cleared, very often the cause of a problem will disappear. Facts only acquire significance and importance *relative* to the question asked. Or, putting it another way, it is the question you frame that turns data into information. It is possible, however, that the significance of a fact does not appear until Stages 3 and 4, when a tentative solution or hypothesis may send the thinker back to Stage 2 for a fact they have overlooked, or even to search for evidence that was not then apparent.

Let me now sum up Stage 2, when your attention is fully focused on the problem. It can be called the *analytic* phase: the situation out of which the difficulty arises is broken up; the problem is isolated and formulated; the various facts and conditions bearing upon it are collected, verified, sorted, arranged and examined; and their significance, simply or in groups, assessed in the light of previous judgments.

Incidentally, some people think of analysis as simply taking things to bits, like a child dismantling a toy. But it is much more than that – when analysing, you are looking for something.

What your quarry actually is will depend on the nature of the case, but you may be:

- Establishing the *relationship* of the parts to each other and to the whole;

- Finding the true *cause* or causes of the problem;

- Identifying the *issue* at stake, the 'either – or' upon which a decision must rest (what a good trial judge does);

- Discovering a *law* in nature;

- Searching for the *principles* behind experience.

3. Suggestion

The third stage is reached when possible solutions – perhaps little more than guesses – to the problem begin to suggest themselves to the thinker, but these may only occur after prolonged consideration of the data and their implications. In fact, this and the previous stage tend to merge: data give rise to suggestions, and suggestions often cause the thinker to make further inquiries with the object of securing more data.

4. Reasoning

There may also be considerable interplay between these last two stages and Stage 4, when the thinker reasons out the consequences of each suggestion in turn. Some suggestions that are little more than guesses may be dropped almost as soon as they occur.

The characteristic that marks Stage 4 is that it usually involves the use of a *hypothetical* form of reasoning. This line of thought begins with a supposition: '*Supposing* X is true, then a, b, c, d or e will surely (or probably) follow.' In other words, the supposition – alias hypothesis – merits some serious consideration as a possible solution. If the a, b, c, d or e consequences that follow correspond with all the relevant data, and if the hypothesis covers and accounts for all the perplexing elements which appeared when the situation was analysed in Stage 2, then that hypothesis is worthy of acceptance in Stage 5 as a reasoned solution of the problem.

The clear thinker will choose a solution objectively according to its tenability in relation to the facts and its power to account for them. The prejudiced person, on the other hand, is over-influenced by their feelings often operating at a subconscious level. They are predisposed to choose the easiest, the most agreeable or the most comfortable solution and to discard what runs counter to their subjective assumptions or preconditions. The lazy person tends to choose the easiest or most comfortable option – the least line of resistance.

5. Conclusion

This stage is reached when the thinker has been able to assemble all the pieces of the jigsaw puzzle into a composite and coherent whole. What at first was an apparently random set of facts, ideas and possibilities has now taken shape and you can see the whole as a picture. Hence it can be called the *synthetic* stage. A *synthesis* is the building up of a complex whole by the union of elements, especially the process of forming concepts, general ideas or theories.

6. Test

In this stage the chosen hypothesis – the provisional solution – is submitted to test or trial before being finally adopted. For example, a controlled experiment in a scientific laboratory – one in which all the ingredients and conditions of a problem are exactly reproduced to see if the proposed solution is repeated – is such a test. Without a successful series of results from such tests, certitude is lacking that the solution arrived at simply by thought is the correct one.

'The greatest uncertainty will prevail where human beings and human relationships provide the raw material of the problem confronting the thinker,' writes Jepson, 'for not only are they infinitely variable and difficult to analyse or classify exhaustively, but they are not easy to weigh, calculate or assess with objective exactitude.'

Strictly speaking, no generalization concerning people or human relationships can ever really be made, only tendencies or propensities identified. At best, such tendencies will serve you as only rough-and-ready guides – or 'rules of thumb' – to future behaviours or happenings. In human affairs the unexpected and the incalculable are always to be reckoned with, and have a habit of turning up when you least expect them, so any general rules and principles need to be applied with caution and due regard to the uniqueness of each person, group and situation.

As you will have gathered by now, judgment is only called for in conditions where considerable uncertainty prevails. You will also have noticed uncertainty is often an excuse for not coming to a conclusion at all, or for refusing to put a conclusion rationally reached to a practical test. Some people when faced ultimately with a choice between two alternatives simply will not commit themselves to one or the other. Either because they fear the unpleasant consequences of being wrong, or because they mistake the attitude of 'sitting on the fence' for one of commendable impartiality.

Of course, there are times when 'sitting on the fence' is the wisest thing to do – it's all a matter of judgment. As a correspondent to the *Sunday Times* wrote on 6 September 1998:

> Sitting on the fence is a much-maligned practice. For one thing, you get a better view. You also keep your feet dry and your options open. Of course, it may not look very elegant, but there are times when refusing to decide shows a firmer purpose than sheepishly climbing down off the railing muttering: 'Oh, all right then, if you insist.'

Others when faced with the consequences of a conclusion that appears to follow from a rational examination of the available facts shrink from putting it to a practical trial on the grounds that 'it's all very well in theory, but it won't work in practice'.

If such are the results of 'thinking' for such people, then it would probably have been better if they had saved themselves the trouble for unless a conclusion is reached and used as the basis of subsequent action or further experiment, thinking is incomplete and its primary object remains unattained.

Those who suspend judgment indefinitely because immediate certainty is not attainable may find themselves in the unenviable position of waiting forever. A Japanese proverb compares such a person to a man who stands on one leg all his life! By contrast, the clear thinker suspends their judgment only as long as the circumstances of their problem permit, and no longer. When the time comes to act, they will act with courage and firmness, even if only on a balance of probabilities. They may be wrong, but in some circumstances, it is better to be wrong than perpetually indecisive.

President Franklin D. Roosevelt had no doubts on that score. 'One thing is sure,' he declared in a speech to Congress shortly after his presidential inauguration during the Great Depression, 'We have to do *something*. We have to do the best we know how at the moment. If it doesn't turn out right, we can modify it as we go along.' The ancient Romans had a useful phrase for this pragmatic approach: *solvitur ambulando* – solve it while you are walking forward.

Judgment is so often a matter of timing. A leader with good judgment will sense when the time is ripe to act. The time for talking is over and the time for action is at hand. Their demeanour should reflect that change.

The leader must not only be decisive; he must impress his followers with the fact that a decision has been reached

and that hesitation, vacillation and questioning are over.
He must act in a decided way and support his decision
with a confident and courageous attitude.
He must look decided.

ORDWAY TEAD, *THE ART OF LEADERSHIP* (1935)

A decision or conclusion is seldom the end of the road: one thing leads to another. Effective thinkers know that there is no contradiction involved in making firm decisions and at the same time preserving a certain openness of mind. They know that their judgments will have to run the gauntlet of time. For new facts and on-going experience are bound to test their decisions or provisional conclusions. They may emerge confirmed or strengthened, or end up on the cutting room floor of history. When it comes to all our judgments, personal or collective, the proof of the pudding is in the eating.

* * * * * * *

Thinking to some purpose – the process outlined in this chapter – is not restricted to any particular field of study or domain of work, it is common to all of them and available to all. Knowledge, theoretical or practical, is arguably ultimately all one: thinking is the interchangeable handle to the tools used in its various branches.

Although no two individuals may behave in precisely the same way – just as no two battles may follow precisely the same course or include exactly similar incidents – nevertheless, when one looks not at the details but at the general patterns and outcomes, then it is possible to study human thinking and judgment abstractly.

Key points: Thinking to some purpose

- When your mind is thinking to some purpose there are three major functions or families of mental skills that come into play: *analysing*, *synthesizing* and *valuing*;

- *Analysing* is essentially separating, dissecting or taking things apart to see what they are made of. *Synthesizing* is essentially putting things together, assembling, joining up. *Valuing* is essentially assessing the worth of something according to some scale of reference;

- When we think we are, so to speak, constantly switching from one 'musical key' of thinking to another, though we are seldom aware of doing so. For the process is a holistic one, and as such, it is not amenable to introspection;

- The human mind can think purposively on different levels of consciousness. Quite a lot of analysing, synthesizing and valuing is done at a subliminal or less than conscious level. That's another reason why you cannot inspect your judgment when it is at work, as if you are inspecting a machine;

- Emotion or feeling can encourage and fuel effective thinking, for what is interest but a kind of feeling? But negative emotions, especially fear in all its forms – especially diffused anxiety – have mostly bad effects on the process of judgment. You cannot command your feelings but you can command your attention. Measure your fears but don't dwell on them. In other words, resolve to stay positive;

- Knowledge of the range, depth and capability of our own mind is in fact your only gateway to knowledge of all other human minds, not least those of your colleagues at work. You know yourself, so to speak, from the inside; all others only from the outside by your five senses. But it is a good working assumption that all our 'insides' have a lot in common;

- We are continually selecting from the information presented, interpreting it with information received in the past and making predictions about the future. When it comes to the skills of doing that, good is good, better is better;

- For what it is worth, the best short definition of judgment that I have come across appears in the 1934 edition of *Webster's Dictionary*: 'the making of a decision or conclusion on the basis of indications and probabilities when the facts are not clearly ascertained'.

Turn him to any cause of policy,
The Gordian knot of it he will unloose,
Familiar as his garter.

WILLIAM SHAKESPEARE, *HENRY V*, ACT I, SCENE I

2

Decision-making

Thinking begins in what may fairly enough be called
a forked-road situation: a situation which is ambiguous,
which presents a dilemma, which proposes alternatives.

JOHN DEWEY

WHAT IS DECISION? By giving the victory to one side or the other, you 'cut off' the mental process of weighing both sides – or all angles – of a question, controversy or cause. A decision (from the Latin verb *decidere*, to cut off) means literally that cut-off point where judgment ends and action begins.

Note that the word implies some form of preliminary confusion or hesitation. Where there is no choice involved – no *forked-road* situation – we do not have the feeling of really making a decision. If you want to get work and you are offered only one job, there is hardly a decision to be made. But if there are two equally inviting offers, then you *are* in the decision-making situation.

The decision-making process does follow a logical pattern, at least in theory. Here is a useful framework:

FIVE-POINT PLAN	
Steps	**Key Actions**
Define objective	Specifying the aim or objective, having recognized the need for a decision.
Collect information	Collecting and organizing data, checking facts and opinions, identifying possible causes, establishing time constraints and other criteria.
Develop options	Listing possible courses of action, generating ideas.
Evaluate and decide	Listing the pros and cons, examining the consequences, measuring against criteria, trials, testing against objective, selecting the best.
Implement	Acting to carry out the decision, monitoring the decision, reviewing.

There are also some even simpler forms, which you may find easier to remember. For example, during a 'Developing Creative Engineers' programme in which I was involved, two participants came up with this useful four-point outline:

1   Definition of the problem;

2   Manipulation of elements bearing on solution;

3 Period resulting in an intuitive idea;

4 The idea is shaped to practical usefulness.

To give you one more example, the Australian Army produced a simple and more memorable form of the traditional but far more complex military guide to decision-making, known as the 'Appreciation of the Situation'.

Aim	*What am I/we to achieve?*
Factors	*What will hinder or help me/us?*
Courses	*What could I/we or the other parties* do in light of these factors? (*competitors, enemy, customers, etc., depending on your business)*
Plan	*What will I/we do?*

No person in their right senses sets out intentionally to make mistakes. All of us will benefit from having a simple checklist at hand to ensure that we remain in the flight path of the effective decision. Here are some key questions to consider for your own checklist:

- Have I defined the objective?

- Do I have sufficient information?

- What are the feasible options?

- Have I evaluated them correctly?

- Does this decision feel right, now I have begun to implement it?

When you do make a mistake, turn it to your profit. Go back to your checklist and try to identify precisely where you went wrong, then you will be learning by experience. This in turn helps to programme your own personal computer – your subconscious mind. The next time, the red light that precedes a potential mistake will flash sooner.

Be disciplined or systematic

One of the functions of a leader is to prevent a group from 'putting the cart before the horse': jumping to a conclusion or decision without fully understanding the problem. Experienced decision-makers learn to be suspicious of premature consensus and either/or thinking. Peter Drucker, the eminent management writer, declared provocatively: 'The first rule in decision-making is that one does not make a decision unless there is disagreement,' and he illustrated his point with this story:

Albert P. Sloan [former head of General Motors] is reported to have said at a meeting of one of his top committees:

'Gentlemen, I take it we are all in complete agreement on the decision here.' Everyone around the table nodded assent.

'Then,' continued Mr Sloan, 'I propose we postpone further discussion of this matter until our next meeting to give ourselves time to develop disagreement and perhaps gain some understanding of what the decision is all about.'

* * * * * * *

The arbitrary or illogical inversion of the order can be made comical by an imaginative writer. Lewis Carroll did so in the closing chapters of *Alice in Wonderland*, where he narrates the trial of the Knave of Hearts for stealing tarts baked by the Queen:

'Let the jury consider their verdict,' the King said, for about the twentieth time that day.

'No, No!' said the Queen. 'Sentence first – verdict afterward.'

'Stuff and nonsense!' said Alice loudly. 'The idea of having the sentence first!'

'Hold your tongue!' said the Queen, turning purple.

'I won't,' said Alice.

'Off with her head!' the Queen shouted at the top of her voice. Nobody moved.

'Who cares for you?' said Alice. (She had grown to her full
size by this time.) 'You're nothing but a pack of cards!'

Develop a proper range of options

Options and alternatives are commonly used as synonyms
these days, but there is a useful distinction between them, one
well worth remembering. An *alternative* is, strictly speaking, a
mutually exclusive choice of two available things; an *option* is a
choice between more than two such things.

Having established the truth to the best of your ability, you
are then in a position to generate and choose between possible
courses of action or solutions, here called *options*. By the end of
it you should have a clear idea of the structure of options and
know how to manage the process of selecting from them the best
one for your purpose.

It is important in this phase to understand what you are
seeking. You are not trying to identify *all* the possibilities
of action. That step, so often recommended in management
textbooks, is a recipe for indecision. Take chess. You might
assume that a computer can look at every possible move in the
game, but that is not so. A very ordinary game will run to 25
moves, and if a computer wants to consider every possibility

equally as the game proceeds, it has to consider 1,000 followed by 75 noughts combinations of moves!

Now, suppose that computers could consider a million moves a second, it would still take them longer than the entire history of our planetary system for them to sort out all the possibilities. Therefore, a sensible computer – like you or me – only looks a few moves ahead. The computer's weakness here lies in its lack of a *valuing* faculty. The chess master knows at once which moves are *feasible*, namely the ones worth considering. And that is a value judgment.

The word *feasible* is crucially important because it saves you time. When it comes to scanning options, it helps immeasurably if you know what you are looking for. *Possible* is a much wider term embracing everything that could be done within the limits of the situation, whereas *feasible* narrows it down a little to what can be done with existing resources and fits the success criteria, which – in real life as opposed to chess – will certainly include values.

The first thing to do is to sort out the feasible options from the greater number of possible options. Imagine yourself as a coin dealer or a diamond merchant sifting quickly through someone's collection and choosing the five or six specimens worth considering for purchase. Then you need to proceed by *elimination*. So the process resembles a cone, as shown in this funnel-shaped model:

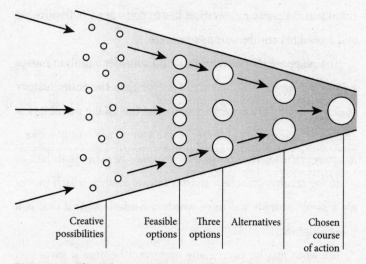

Figure 2.1 *The Lobster Pot Model of decision-making*

It is common sense, as well as scientific orthodoxy now, that it is easier to disprove things than to prove them. Theoretically, you cannot prove anything finally and conclusively, but for practical purposes you can, in so far as your approximation to truth is near enough for everyday needs. Science is constantly trying to devise tests to support or disprove hypotheses. All that a truthful scientist can say about a hypothesis is that it has survived all those tests up to this date.

As Albert Einstein replied to a woman who was congratulating him on news of an astronomical observation that seemed to prove his theory of relativity: 'Madam, a thousand experiments cannot ever prove me right, a single experiment can prove me wrong.' Your aim in working on the feasible options is to reduce them to two alternatives – either this or that – as soon as possible. But remember the proverb: *More haste, less speed*.

The experienced practical thinker dislikes situations indicated by the acronym TINA – 'There is no alternative.' If you stop to look and think hard enough, there usually is one.

THE BRIDGE OF DEATH

IT WAS 17 SEPTEMBER 1862. Cannon thundered along the battle lines as two armies of Blue and Grey soldiers faced each other across the Antietam Creek. Then General Ambrose Burnside gave the order to advance. The Union army was to storm across the creek and attack the enemy at close quarters. The route he chose to send them led over the narrow bridge across the creek, the only one in the vicinity. The Confederate gunners in the batteries specially placed to command the bridge could hardly believe their eyes. They swept away regiment after regiment with grapeshot. The slaughter was appalling.

General Burnside had failed to discover that the Antietam Creek in this region was only about three feet deep. It could have been forded by infantry or cavalry at any point with perfect safety.

Burnside acted on the assumption that he had only one option open to him. In fact, we now know that he was wrong. He had not carried out a thorough reconnaissance, and his decision rested upon an erroneous understanding of his situation.

Of the battle at Antietam and the general who lost it for him, President Lincoln said somewhat bitterly: 'Only he could have wrung so spectacular a defeat from the jaws of victory.'

It is also an all-too-common error of judgment to jump quickly from five or six feasible options to just two: the either/or alternatives.

Adolf Hitler had a penchant for doing just that. Intuitive thinkers – especially if they believe themselves divinely gifted in that department – tend to jump to the either/or situation without apparently going through a conscious process of considering and eliminating a wide range of options. Albert Speer, one of Hitler's key ministers and intimates, noted this tendency. Hitler's domestic staff even joked openly about it to the dictator's face, apparently without incurring his wrath. Thus, his standard phrase, 'There are two possibilities', would be used by one of his secretaries, in his presence, often in the most everyday context. She would say, for example, 'There are two possibilities. Either it is going to rain or it is not going to rain.'

Hitler's failure to think systematically about military situations, compounded by a growing distrust of those generals and staff officers around him who could do so, plus the effects of sustained emotional stress upon his mental capacity, lost him the Second World War. He would have done better to remember the wise words of Prussian statesman Otto von Bismarck: 'When your enemy has only two options open to him, you can be sure that he will choose the third.'

In fact, it's not a bad policy to work on the assumption that feasible options can – more often than not – be reduced to just three runners in the race, an application of the so-called 'Rule of Three'.

The Rule of Three

Our brains evolved in a way to protect us from harm. As part of our protection system, we like to have choices. We know that if we don't have a choice in a dangerous situation, we may not find a way out of it. On the other hand, our brains also know that if we have too many choices, we often get confused. If we are confused, we may make the wrong choice, which could cause us serious harm. This means that the brain likes to have choices, but not too many choices.

You may recall the children's story of *Goldilocks and the Three Bears*, where the heroine – a young girl with golden hair – finds herself in the kitchen of the bears' house, feeling hungry. She has a choice between three bowls of the bears' porridge on the table, with not a bear in sight or sound. Which shall she choose to eat? Three choices enable us to avoid the ones that are too hot and too cold, too big and too small, and select the one that is just right.

Our natural predilection for three is reflected in our language. Universally, all languages are based on three elements and are constant: *subject–verb–object*. They are commonly in that order (the exception to the rule being the Burmese language, where the object comes first). Still on language, notice that English assigns importance to the first three numbers by giving them unique endings – 1st, 2nd and 3rd. For numbers that follow, they all have the same ending – 4th, 5th, 6th, 7th, etc.

The Olympics and other sporting events provide further proof of the rule or power of the number three. Here, the winner of an event wins the Gold medal. The athlete who comes second gets the Silver, and the one that is third receives the Bronze. There is no medal for fourth, fifth, or beyond. In so many contests, people stop counting after third place. The human mind seems either not to care or not remember who comes in beyond third.

If you consider colour, light refracts into three primary colours – red, green and blue. In terms of pigments, the three primary colours are red, yellow and blue. And, in music, the third note of every scale provides the most basic harmony that human ears find pleasing, while musical triads are the building blocks of musical harmony. Lastly, those well versed in geometry know that a triangle with three sides is the most stable shape. This is why bridges and buildings that must carry a lot of weight have structural elements based on triangles. And there are just three shapes of triangles: isosceles, scalene and equilateral. Lastly, whether fact or fiction, all stories have a three-fold framework of a *beginning*, *middle* and *end*.

Assuming our minds are natural pattern-seekers, constantly looking for relationships and meanings in the world around us, three is actually the smallest number we need to create a pattern. It gives us the perfect combination of brevity and rhythm. The Romans expressed it, appropriately enough, in a concise Latin phrase of just three words: *omne trium perfectum* (everything that comes in threes is perfect, or, every set of three is complete).

The do-nothing option is sometimes worth considering

If neither alternative attracts you, and you cannot produce a satisfactory compromise, it is always worth asking yourself, 'Do I have to take action at all?' The option of doing nothing, of deciding not to act, is always worth considering. Sometimes the proposed cure promises to be worse than the disease. At other times, you may sense that if left alone there is a good chance that time will satisfactorily solve the problem of its own accord. But the decision to do nothing must be taken for good reason and not simply because you have 'thrown in the towel'.

Only by judging the consequences of doing nothing can we transform it into a positive course of action. Decisions are like surgery, carrying with them the setting up of all kinds of chain reactions in the living organisms of relationships, organizations and societies. Even if the decision is a minor one it can always cause a mild degree of shock. Sometimes the organism might survive the shock and benefit from the surgical operation, at other times a decision might finish it off. In the latter case the remedy will most certainly be worse than the disease.

In retrospect

We do not succeed in changing things according to our desire, but gradually our desire changes. The situation that we hoped to change because it was intolerable becomes unimportant. We have not managed to surmount the obstacle, as we were absolutely determined to do, but life has taken us round it, led us past it, and then if we turn round to gaze at the remote past, we can barely catch sight of it, so imperceptible has it become.

MARCEL PROUST (1871–1922)

As a variation, if there is no obvious winner, nor a trade-off between objective achievement and implementability, you may wish to choose the option that is most likely to keep your options open. The policy of keeping options open for as long as possible has much to recommend it.

Options checklist

Constantly ask yourself and your colleagues these questions:

- Which possibilities are feasible, given our limitations?
- Which of the feasible options are the true alternatives?
- Are they mutually exclusive, or can we do

    (a) Both, *or*

    (b) Some creative combination of the two?
- Will the resulting compromise achieve our objective better than either of the discrete courses?
- Would it be better to do nothing?
- In what circumstances should we abandon the policy of keeping our options open for as long as possible?

You may object, saying often there is insufficient time to work steadily through the cone, but even in the tensest situations, it is best to keep your head and mentally check out the most likely possibilities.

False assumptions – or, walking on very thin ice

Once you have acquired some knowledge about the apparent limits or limitations in a problem or situation, you should test them for reality. This is value thinking: are they real or true limits, or are they false ones? Finding out may require some physical work. Had he carried out a proper reconnaissance, General Burnside (*see page* 35) would have discovered that Antietam Creek was not a real limitation to the movement of soldiers. Far from being a boundary, it was an open gateway.

Military history abounds with examples of generals exploiting the infinite capacity of the human mind to make false assumptions about limits. Before his invasion of Italy early in his career, Emperor Napoleon Bonaparte (1769–1821) read the works of many writers who repeated that it was impracticable to consider crossing the Alps in winter with a large army. His staff officers agreed. But Napoleon always thought for himself, and he challenged that view:

> The winter is not the most unfavourable season for the passage of lofty mountains. The snow is then firm, the weather settled,

and there is nothing to fear from avalanches, the real and only danger to be apprehended in the Alps. On those high mountains, there are often very fine days in December, of a dry cold, with extreme calmness in the air.

Hitler made a similar decision in 1940 when he brushed aside the received conclusion of the German General Staff that it would be impossible to take armoured divisions through the wooded hills of the Ardennes – and on this occasion was proved right.

A COSTLY STRATEGIC ERROR OF JUDGMENT

IN THE 1930S THE BRITISH Imperial General Staff spent much time resolving how to defend Britain's colonies in the Far East. They fortified the island of Singapore as a bastion, constructing powerful batteries of heavy guns to make it impregnable from the sea and a great naval base to shelter the fleet that would be sent there in wartime. Little time was spent on the possibility that Singapore would be attacked by land across the causeway joining it to the mainland. The British military planners assumed that the mountainous jungle of Malaya was impassable to a modern army. Nor did they spend much money on air defences, for the admirals were convinced that aircraft could not pose much threat to warships.

In 1941 the plan was put into action. Two battleships, the *Prince of Wales* and the *Repulse*, were despatched to the Far East to overawe the Japanese. To the surprise of the British generals, however, the Japanese did not land obligingly in front of the British guns but in the north on the mainland. The two British battleships sailed to intercept the invasion fleet but were both sunk by Japanese aircraft. The Japanese struck south through the jungle with ease, and attacked Singapore from the landward side. As the large guns were all pointing the wrong way, the city fell within days and 10,000 British and Australian soldiers became prisoners. In Winston Churchill's words, it was 'the largest capitulation in British history'.

Decision implies real choice. The more feasible options within the broad constraints of time and space you have to choose from, the better your decision is likely to be. Even if there appears to be one course open once the truth has been established, an experienced manager will cast around in their mind to see if there is not another option. By closing thought down too early, the good option can become the enemy of the best option.

Here, imaginative thinking comes into its own. We must draw a sharp distinction between *unconscious* assumptions (which may, of course, be true or untrue) and the *conscious* assumptions or suppositions that we can use as a kind of portable stepladder in imaginative thinking:

Supposing we had an extra million pounds, what would we do then?

Let us *assume* that the trade union will not object to this plan, how would we implement it?

Assuming, for the moment, that the Board agreed…

KENNEDY AND THE BAY OF PIGS

LOOKING BACK ON THE ABORTIVE invasion of Cuba – the Bay of Pigs fiasco – the then Secretary of State, Dean Rusk, recalled that President John F. Kennedy had conceived a totally unrealistic idea of what a puny brigade of Cuban exiles could possibly achieve. 'I should have told the President,' said Rusk, 'that we might want to do it with American forces. "Ask your military chiefs of staff," I should have said to him, "to assume that American troops would be used. Then get them to tell you what they must have before they invaded Cuba – what air support, ground divisions and naval back-up." If we had made that assumption, we should never have made such an error.'

Creative imagination comes more into play, however, when thinking about how to use existing resources. Your mind can easily become dominated by what some psychologists have called *functional fixedness*, the tendency to see things in association with a given function. The conventional mind accepts these sorts of assumptions: a hammer is for hammering in nails, an army camp is for housing soldiers – if there are no more soldiers, knock it down. Children, before they acquire functional fixedness, are much more imaginative in their play. An object for them can take on any number of uses. The way holiday camps came into being provides an excellent example of creative imagination at work:

Billy Butlin was a circus man. While looking over disused army camps in 1946 he conceived the idea of using them as holiday camps. He even kept the army's tannoy system he found in the camps. He was told it wouldn't work, but Butlin's Holiday Camps played a major part in meeting the needs of the British people, especially before the era of cheap overseas holiday packages.

In imaginative thinking intended to overcome functional fixedness it is useful to remember the principle of artificially restraining or disciplining the critical, analytical, reasoning function. Make the analysers wait their turn. Let your mind off its habitual leashes so that it roams freely wherever it wills to go in the field you have chosen.

Weighing up consequences

The game of consequences lies at the heart of the rational approach to decision-making. But consequences, when you examine them carefully, are not susceptible to precise calculation. As a principle, the more familiar a situation is to you, the more you will be able to judge its consequences. Alternatively, someone else's experience may give you clues, which is why history is so important. The newer the situation, the less likely you are to be able to predict consequences.

Now all situations are partly old or familiar (at least to someone else, if not to you), and partly unique. History both does and does not repeat itself. You can see how difficult it then becomes to predict outcomes.

In 1965 the Americans decided to mount a strategic bombing offensive against the North Vietnamese forces, so they had to build airbases near Saigon in the south. To protect these bases, they sent 3,000 marines. But the US Marine Corps is trained to be aggressive. Rather than sit around their perimeters, the commanders on the ground decided on a policy of active defence and defined their objective in terms of confronting the Vietcong. Soon, more soldiers had to be transported there to support them. And more... And more...

Slipshod thinking of this kind about consequences is all too common. After such events the argument becomes a matter of historical judgment: could the Americans have foreseen such results, or ought they to have done so? These are questions of responsibility and blame, involving our powers to make some often very fine distinctions between reasons and excuses. It is better to think thoroughly about probable and possible consequences in advance: the more that can be identified the better. Nowadays, in addition, we are much more aware of the possibility of *unintended* consequences. A classic example, one that affects us all, is the climate change we call 'global warming'.

GOOD AND BAD COMPROMISES

ONE KIND OF COMPROMISE IS expressed in the old proverb 'Half a loaf is better than no bread.' The other kind is expressed in the story of the Judgment of Solomon, a story from the Hebrew bible. Solomon, King of Israel *c.* 930 BCE, was noted for his wisdom and justice. This is evidenced in the case where two women claim the same baby. Solomon offers to cut it in half, thereby prompting the true mother to renounce her claim in order to preserve the child.

In the first instance, the boundary conditions are still being satisfied. The purpose of bread is to provide food, and half a loaf is still food. Half a baby, however, does not satisfy the boundary conditions. For half a baby is not half of a living and growing child, it is a corpse in two pieces.

There is a danger that the more your mind unravels possible consequences, the less likely you are to do anything. Fortunately for us, we cannot foresee all the obvious and hidden consequences of all the options open to us at any one time: we have to take some sort of a risk. In business decisions it is usually the case that the larger the risk, the greater is the potential gain. That principle is always worth bearing in mind. Risk-taking seems to be inseparable from decision-making. So what are the guidelines?

The chief principle is that risks should be taken only after being carefully calculated. This means you will have to make a very thorough effort, using your imagination as well as all the relevant methods of quantification, to calculate as precisely as possible the nature and degree of the risks involved. Then you will be in a position to see what can be done to minimize the risks by prudent foresight and contingency planning. American oil tycoon J. Paul Getty once said: 'When I go into any business deal my chief thoughts are on how I'm going to save myself if things go wrong.'

The proposed benefits should warrant the risk. A successful investment banker, for example, will ensure that on his ventures of capital, the upside potential for him is far in excess of the downside risk. If he gets it right on any given proposition, his investment and bank will make many times its original stake. Even if an investment is a complete failure, as long as he or she has exercised proper care, the bank should still lose no more than the money it invested. The critical factor is always to get the odds right on each investment and only to invest when the upside potential is high in relation to the initial sum advanced.

Knowing that you can accept the precisely predicted consequences of failure is a sign that you have properly explored the risk element of a decision. Ask yourself, what's the worst possible outcome? Am I prepared to accept it, if necessary? Both asking and answering those two questions will greatly ease the task of making a difficult decision.

The various systematic ways of exploring the outcomes of alternative courses of action, using diagrams and mathematical calculations of the odds, are taught in business schools. While I doubt more than one in ten managers ever make use of them in work situations, the principle of exploring probabilities as far as possible is sound. These days, exploring the probabilities of each outcome can often be greatly aided by computers. But computers should never make up your mind for you.

A man may prophesy,
With a near aim, of the main chance of things
As yet not come to life, which in their seeds
And weak beginnings lie intreasured
WILLIAM SHAKESPEARE, *HENRY IV*

Remember, you are always dealing with estimated probabilities. Therefore, results will depend on how good you are at that form of judgment. Even where genuine doubts about estimates exist, however, it is at least useful to be able to examine them as thoroughly as possible.

THE EFFECTIVE DECISION-MAKER

HE WILL NOT RUSH into a decision unless he is sure he understands it. Like any reasonable experienced adult, he has learned to pay attention to what Socrates called his 'daemon': the inner voice, someplace in the bowels, that whispers: 'Take care.'

Just because something is difficult, disagreeable, or frightening is no reason for not doing it, if it is right. But one holds back – if only for a moment – if one finds oneself uneasy, perturbed, bothered without quite knowing why: 'I always stop when things seem out of focus,' is the way one of the best decision-makers of my acquaintance puts it.

Nine times out of ten the uneasiness turns out to be some silly detail. But the tenth time, one suddenly realizes that one has overlooked the most important fact in the problem, has made an elementary blunder, or misjudged altogether...

But the effective decision-maker does not wait long – a few days, at the most a few weeks. If the 'daemon' has not spoken by then, he acts with speed and energy, whether he likes it or not.

Executives are not paid for doing things they like to do. They are being paid for getting the right things done – most of all in their specific task, the making of effective decisions.

PETER DRUCKER, *THE EFFECTIVE EXECUTIVE* (1967)

This thinking – partly analytical, partly valuing – should give way to creative thinking if it is felt necessary to generate some new options. Here, you and your colleagues need to be able to suspend judgment so that the dogs of criticism do not tear every new born idea to shreds.

Chester I. Barnard, who wrote an influential book on *The Functions of the Executive* (1938) when he was president of the New Jersey Bell Telephone Company, concluded with this masterly summary:

The fine art of executive decision consists in not deciding questions that are not now pertinent, in not deciding prematurely, in not making decisions that cannot be made effective, and in not making decisions that others should make.

Key points: Decision-making

- Notice the word *options* rather than *alternatives*. An *alternative* is literally one of two courses open. Decision-makers who lack skill tend to jump far too quickly to the *either/or* of alternatives. They do not give enough time and mental energy to generating at least three or four possibilities;

- You need to open your mind into wide focus to consider all possibilities and that is where creative thinking comes in. But then your valuing faculty needs to come into play to narrow it down to the feasible options – the ones that may or can be done, the practicable ones;

- When considering options, remember it tends to be easier to discard an option rather than to embrace it. In other words, we are often better at knowing what we don't want to do rather than what we *do* want to do;

- Also while reviewing options, ask yourself constantly whether or not you are overlooking some feasible course of action, perhaps because it is just too obvious;

- Always check your assumptions: the less hidden they are, the better. For if they are known to you, their applicability to *this* situation is much easier to assess;

- As a general principle, if you accumulate enough information then you should not have to make a conscious decision. For the decision will, as we say, make itself. If that happens, you will find that you are wholehearted about it.

Men sleep well in the Inn of Decision.
ARAB PROVERB

3

Experience – the seedbed

Experience is by industry achiev'd
And perfected by the swift course of time.

WILLIAM SHAKESPEARE, *TWO GENTLEMEN OF VERONA*,
ACT I, SCENE III

EXPERIENCE AND JUDGMENT are not exact synonyms, though people sometimes talk as if they are. The two concepts are deeply interrelated but they are definitely not the same thing. As the philosopher Michel de Montaigne said: 'Judgment can do without knowledge, but not knowledge without judgment.'

Without some growth in judgment, experience signifies nothing more than a mere piling up of involvements. In its fullest sense, however, knowledge – the familiarity or understanding gained by experience or study or instruction – is the seedbed of good judgment. The American–British writer Henry James lists among its flowers or fruits:

> …the power to guess the unseen from the seen, to trace the implication of things, to judge the whole piece by the pattern, the condition of feeling life in general so completely that you are well on your way to knowing any particular corner of it – this cluster of gifts may almost be said to constitute experience.

POPULAR HISTORICAL WRITERS – NOT experienced historians – have sometimes called the British infantry on the Western Front in the First World War 'lions led by donkeys'. The phrase dates back to a French general's comment about the British in the Crimean War of the mid-nineteenth century, where it was more appropriate.

Donkeys don't learn from their involvements. Marshal Maurice de Saxe was a famous mercenary general in the eighteenth century. He owned a donkey that carried his personal baggage on 20 campaigns. 'Marshal Saxe's donkey' became a byword – a thing cited as a notable example – for generals whose long experience of war had still left them devoid of seasoned military judgment.

Normally, however, experience derived from long practical immersion in a particular field or domain of work *does* imply superior understanding. We expect far more from an experienced sea captain, surgeon or professor than from their novice counterparts. In other words, we tend to assume – usually correctly – that participation over time in their chosen form has developed their powers of judgment.

The key factor here is a simple one: judgment is cumulative. After any particular exercise of judgment there is always some feedback which, consciously or subconsciously, enters the mind and informs any future essays in decision-making. Our choices tend to get better.

As the eminent British philosopher G.E. Moore – a great intellectual defender of common sense – observed in *Principia Ethica* (1903): 'We are all, I think, in this strange position that we do *know* many things… and yet we do not know *how* we know them.' You will know if a particular new pair of shoes is right for your feet. A cobbler, by contrast, may know the material and design requirements of a good pair of shoes. He has *technical* knowledge, you have *tacit* knowledge. Judgment – how to exercise it – is a form of *tacit* knowledge.

Judgment as intuitive decision-making

Through distilled and refined experience – the product of reflection – a seasoned individual's judgment becomes a virtually spontaneous knowledge of what to do or what *not* to do. You will just know what will work, and often just when and just how to do it. Judgment, then, is the product at subconscious level of all those years of consciously following the rational procedures of judging and deciding that I reminded you of in the first two chapters of this book.

As we have seen, judgment stemming from experience is most called for when a high level of uncertainty exists, when the facts are not easy to ascertain, and above all, when time is limited and there is immense pressure to make the right decision quickly.

All these factors characterize what we call a crisis situation. In the extreme form of crisis, not only is the time for decision short but also life-or-death is at stake. Such circumstances in certain fields can provide a supreme test of professional judgment and skill.

THE MIRACLE OF THE HUDSON

ON 15 JANUARY 2009, US Airways Flight 1549 was struck by a flock of Canada geese shortly after take-off from LaGuardia Airport, New York. The bird strike rendered both engines on the Airbus A320 inoperative.

In an incredible feat of judgment and professional skill in the context of impending disaster, pilot Chesley 'Sully' Sullenberger took the decision to land the stricken plane on the Hudson River. All 150 passengers and five crew were rescued from the plane as it floated intact on the river. After the incident Sullenberger modestly told CBS News anchor Katie Courie, 'One way of looking at this might be that, for 42 years, I've been making small regular deposits in this bank of experience, education and training and on January 15, the balance was sufficient so that I could make a very large withdrawal.'

Chesley Sullenberger's metaphor of 'small regular deposits in this bank of experience, education and training' is as good an indication as any of the way that good judgment grows in a cumulative or holistic way in a person's whole mind. Although those whose occupations lie in certain fields – such as the military, medical, police or rescue services – are trained for such emergencies, those elements that go to the making of judgment are equally present in business or politics. It is as if your subconscious mind enlists itself in doing the necessary work for you.

PRACTICAL INTUITION

HOTELIER CONRAD HILTON (1887–1979) WAS once trying to buy an old hotel in Chicago whose owners promised to sell to the highest bidder. Several days before the deadline date for sealed bids, Hilton submitted a hastily made $165,000 offer. He went to bed that night feeling vaguely disturbed and woke the next morning with a hunch that his bid was not high enough. 'That didn't feel right to me,' he later wrote. 'Another figure kept coming, 180,000 dollars. It satisfied me. It seemed fair. It felt right. I changed my bid to the larger figure on that hunch. When they were opened the closest bid to mine was 179,000 dollars.'

Can you think of a similar incident in your career so far?

Hilton was fortunate in that he still had time to change his decision, nor was he hooked on the notion that once you have made a decision, it shows want of character to change your mind. It may do *after* your point of no return, but not *before* it. As a proverb says, *A wise man changes his mind, a fool never.*

How judgment develops in business

By making a conscious effort to review experience you can develop your purposive subconscious mind into a formidable instrument. Trusting it is important. You should also develop a special kind of inward sensitivity, so that you can pick up the delicate signals; that thought which stirs imperceptibly like a leaf touched by the air, telling you that something is moving. As Conrad Hilton wrote: 'I know when I have a problem and have done all I can to figure it, I keep listening in a sort of inside silence until something clicks and I feel a right answer.'

We owe the classic descriptions of the subconscious mind at work in business decisions to Lord Roy Thomson, the Canadian press magnate. In his autobiography, *After I was Sixty* (Hamish Hamilton, 1975), he mused on the impulses and skills that led him to successfully pursue his distinguished business career long after most of his contemporaries had retired:

I must now ask myself: what was it that gave me this self-confidence, this determination and adventurous spirit in business… at 67?

It was at last partly due to my discovery over a fairly long period, but more than ever during these latter years in Edinburgh and London, that experience was a very important element in the management side of business and it was, of course, the one thing that I had plenty of. I could go further and say that for management to be good it generally must be experienced. To be good at anything at all requires a lot of practice, and to be really good at *making* decisions you have to have plenty of practice at taking decisions. The more one is exposed to the necessity of making decisions, the better one's decision-making becomes.

At various times during my business life I have had to take some important decisions and, particularly in the early days, I often got these wrong. But I found later that the early mistakes and, for that matter, the early correct decisions, stood me in good stead. Most of the problems that I was confronted with in London were in one way or another related to those earlier ones. It was often a matter of just adding some zeros to figures and the sums were the same. In a great many instances I knew the answer immediately.

I cannot explain this scientifically, but I was entirely convinced that, through the years, in my brain as in a computer, I had stored details of the problems themselves, the decisions reached and the results obtained; everything was neatly filed away there for future use.

Then, later, when a new problem arose, I would think it over and, if the answer was not immediately apparent, I would let it go for a while, and it was as if it went the rounds of the brain cells looking for guidance that could be retrieved, for by next morning, when I examined the problem again, more often than not the solution came up right away.

That judgment seemed to be come to almost unconsciously, and my conviction is that during the time I was not consciously considering the problem, my subconscious had been turning it over and relating it to my memory; it had been held up to the light of the experiences I had had in past years and the way through the difficulties became obvious. I am pretty sure other older men had had this same evidence of the brain's subconscious work.

This makes it all very easy, you may say. But, of course, it doesn't happen easily. That bank of experience from which I was able to draw in the later years was not easily funded...

Thinking is work. In the early stages of a man's career it is very hard work. When a difficult decision or problem arises, how easy it is, after looking at it superficially, to give up thinking about it. It is easy to put it from one's mind. It is easy to decide that it is insoluble, or that something will turn up to help us. Sloppy and inconclusive thinking becomes a habit. The more one does it the more one is unfitted to think a problem through to a proper conclusion.

If I have any advice to pass on, as a successful man, it is this: if one wants to be successful, one must think; one must think until it hurts. One must worry a problem in one's mind until it seems there cannot be another aspect of it that hasn't been considered. Believe me, that is hard work and, from my close observation, I can say that there are few people indeed who are prepared to perform this arduous and tiring work.

But let me go further and assure you of this: while, in the early stages, it is hard work and one must accept it as such, later one will find that it is not so difficult, the thinking apparatus has become trained; it is trained even to do some of the thinking subconsciously as I have shown. The pressure that one had to use on one's poor brain in the early stages no longer is necessary; the hard grind is rarely needed; one's mental computer arrives at decisions instantly or during a period when the brain seems to be resting. It is only the rare and most complex problems that require the hard toil of protracted mental effort.

What is 'one's mental computer' actually doing in those depths hidden from our prying eyes? It is almost certainly *analysing*, *synthesizing* and *valuing*.

The subconscious mind's work of *analysing* can be compared to your stomach, which is fed with powerful enzymes that can break down the meals it is given. The analogy of digestion, the process of making food absorbable by dissolving it and breaking it down into simpler chemical compounds, seems especially apt. As the eminent psychologist C.A. Mace wrote: 'As food requires to be assimilated and built into the system, so does knowledge. What has been learned requires consolidation. There is also a process of analysis and re-synthesis in thought which is, so to speak, the metabolism of the mind. Relatively little of what we learn do we need to retain in its original form. Some reorganization is required, some individual synthesis relevant to our private intellectual ends.'

With regard to *valuing*, it is again impossible to be precise about what goes on. What is clear, however, is that our values inhabit our deeper mind and are often obscure to us until we do something or have to choose between two alternatives.

Rationally, we may believe (quite rightly) that decisions should be made on the basis of our values. It is often the case, however, that the decision comes first and then it tells us something about what our values really are.

There is another related phenomenon here, namely that the act of decision in itself somehow confers value – 'Because I have chosen Smith as branch manager therefore he must be good.' That tendency is one that I suggest you should monitor carefully!

Some takeaway points

- *Look on your brain as a mental computer*

  Earlier sequences of decisions and results are fed into
  the mind. Where solutions are not easily apparent, allow
  time for your subconscious mind to work on it. As a
  principle, a period of close enquiry and reflection should
  be followed either by a change of subject or a period
  of inactivity;

- *Shun mental laziness*

  At all stages of your career, conscious thinking demands
  some very hard work. You have to be prepared for that
  effort. If you do so when young, you will reap the benefit
  of an exceptionally good subconscious mind;

- *Few people are willing to make the effort*

  That is a challenging comment. It could be good news for
  you. As the proverb says, *The many fail, the one succeeds.*

Business flair

'Looking back on my own scientific work,' said Lord Adrian, a
former Nobel Prize winner, 'I should say that it shows no great

originality but a certain amount of business instinct which leads to the selection of a profitable line.'

Instinct, flair and intuition are really all pretty much the same. A person who consistently deploys an instinctive power of discernment in a certain field is said to have flair. They can 'smell' a good prospect or which direction the truth might lie in; rather than reasoning towards their goal step-by-step, they sniff their way there by intuition. Indeed, flair comes from a French verb, '*flairer*', meaning 'to smell'.

Note the following comment from John Paul Getty:

When I first started drilling in the Oklahoma soil, the consensus of expert judgment held that there could be no oil in the so-called Red Beds region. But like so many oilmen, I chose to temper all 'analytical' thinking with a healthy dose of non-logical subjectivity. To me, the area looked as if it might hide oil. Largely on the basis of a hunch, I decided to see for myself. I began drilling in the Red Beds, struck oil and brought in a vast new producing field. I rather suspect that by relying upon such non-textbook thought processes and taking attendant risks, the biggest fortunes have been made – in oil and other endeavours.

Business flair is a consistent theme in the lives of great industrialists and merchants. They intuitively spot an opportunity for making money, they can smell a potential profit where others can see nothing but present losses. It's an instinct separate from the dictates of reason or logic that guide more plodding minds.

If you add to this kind of business flair the willingness to take risks in the employment of capital, you are dealing with an entrepreneur. An entrepreneur can be a sole operator, of course, but more often than not the successful ones set up their own companies or organizations. They now find themselves in the role of being a leader. But despite their gifts of intuition in product developing and innovation, or in business trading situations generally, the entrepreneur may not have good judgment about people. For Nature rarely bestows all its personal talents on one person.

You may not have had the good fortune to work closely with outstanding practical thinkers but you can still learn a great deal from observing and reflecting on the colleagues around you: the senior managers to whom you are responsible, your colleagues and your team members. Don't ignore the latter: they may have had the benefit of more education and professional training than you. Why not profit from it?

The best of all ways of learning good judgment is to serve your apprenticeship as a leader with someone who has it – a true mentor. Alfred Sloan worked with William C. Durant, the founder of General Motors. He recalled that Durant 'would proceed on a course of action guided solely, as far as I could tell, by some intuitive flash of brilliance. He never felt obliged to make an engineering hunt for facts.' Sloan, perhaps the greatest systems manager of his day, correctly concluded from observing Durant, 'the final act of business judgment is intuitive'.

Incidentally, as only you can teach yourself the art of judgment, I recommend that you keep a notebook in which to enter your tentative conclusions, helpful examples, principles, new ideas, proverbs and so on. Make notes from the books or articles you read that have a bearing on the subject. Try to imagine what mental habits you would like to have developed at the end of three years: list them in your book. Go through your notebook carefully every month or so, looking backwards to see what else you have learnt. Think about thinking – it is your profession. Ink is the only memory that never fades.

> 'The horror of that moment,' the King went on, 'I shall never, never forget!'
> 'You will though,' the Queen said, 'if you don't make a memorandum of it.'
>
> LEWIS CARROLL, *THROUGH THE LOOKING GLASS*

Personal intuition

Intuition is the power or faculty of immediately apprehending that something is the case. It apparently occurs without the intervention of any reasoning process. There is no deductive or inductive step-by-step reasoning, no conscious analysis of the situation, no employment of the imagination, just a quick and ready insight – 'I just know.'

'I have no other but a woman's reason,' says Lucetta, Julia's woman-in-waiting in Shakespeare's *Two Gentlemen of Verona* (Act I, Scene II). 'I think him so, because I think him so.' Down the centuries, women have been noted for their powers of intuition. Men have been regarded as the more logical of the two sexes. Would you agree?

How intuitive are you?

Intuition is awareness that a situation exists when reason or logic – if consulted – might say that it was improbable or even impossible for it to do so. Do you have such awareness?

Rarely ☐   Sometimes ☐
Frequently ☐   Never ☐

In your judgment of people do you tend to rely upon first impressions? Are they usually right?

Yes ☐   No ☐

Do you often 'feel' your way to a decision or to the solution of problems?

Yes ☐   No ☐

Do you find it difficult sometimes to explain your intuitions to others?

Yes ☐   No ☐

When your intuitions turn out to be wrong, with hindsight why is this so?

1 _____

2 _____

3 _____

On intuition

Besides the kind of thinking in which we are seeing connections between propositions and relating them to that which they signify, we have also an intuitive kind of knowing in which we have sympathetic insight into the character of a person or the demands of a situation, and as we say, grasp it as a whole, and make a judgment about it, without being able to explain how we should justify it… Intuitive insight is the originative and creative grasp of something still in the unknown depths of being.

DOROTHY EMMET (1904–2000), EMERITUS PROFESSOR OF
PHILOSOPHY, UNIVERSITY OF MANCHESTER

'Sometimes it [intuition] is merely a symptom of anxiety.' Emotion and intuition doubtless have their sources close together in the hinterland of the brain. Indeed, they are probably so close, it is quite possible for the wires to be crossed. The negative emotions of fear and anxiety may express themselves as intuitions. A nervous passenger, for example, may have an intuition that their flight to Paris is doomed to crash and so they transfer to another one.

How your physical condition can affect judgment

One implication is that a thinker who relies heavily upon intuition – as many really effective thinkers do – must be physically and emotionally fit. You only have to have a bad bout of flu to know how it affects your emotions: you may become irritable and more depressed; your focus of interest drops down to your tummy; you feel awful; you may be quite certain you are about to die. It is still remarkable, however, how many politicians and generals are allowed to make decisions when physically sick or mentally exhausted.

Stress and tiredness of mind or body can definitely play havoc with the intuitive thinker's immediate comprehension of the reality of a situation. Mountaineers are aware that the quality of decisions drops dramatically when taken in a state of exhaustion.

If you are tired, stick to thinking logically what to do, and do not expect much from your powers of intuition.

The classic case of the effects of emotional stress, physical sickness and plain tiredness on an intuitive man is the one we have already encountered in the person of Adolf Hitler. As a politician and as a military leader, Hitler had considerable flair. His decision to invade France through the dense forest of the Ardennes was based on a strategic intuition in contrast to the more logical thinking of his opponents and even his own highly rational General Staff. But, by 1945, the effects of war had reduced him to a shadow of his former self. Stress symptoms, such as trembling hands and facial twitches, were visible to all. As he disliked bad news, he surrounded himself with men who filtered information for him. Bad news was dressed up as good news. Gradually Hitler lost touch with reality and increasingly retreated into a private world, symbolized by the underground Führer-bunker of his last weeks. Disturbed by stress and emotion, fed misleading information, his intuition had become both a worthless and a dangerous instrument.

Remember, intuition is not always reliable

A wife notices that her husband's work habits have slightly changed: he is spending more time at the office or away on business trips; he seems to be showing less interest in her; he appears to be more distracted in general. Her intuition tells her that he is having an affair. She begins to search for confirmatory evidence... she even contemplates hiring a private detective.

Intuition, as we have seen, is a way of knowing – or believing you know – that a situation exists when there is insufficient evidence for it. The subconscious mind integrates a number of pieces of data – some absorbed through our senses unconsciously – and forms an intuition that surfaces suddenly or gradually in the surface or conscious mind.

An important principle to apply to intuition is to subject those that come early to the most rigorous and sustained checks. If an intuition comes much later, only after the acquisition of much information or after long experience, coupled with reflection, then it is much more likely to be accurate. Early intuitions can so often be no more than an act of jumping to conclusions. And, as mentioned above, they can be so easily fed by those subterranean sources of fear and anxiety lurking within us all.

So, in reality, was that woman's husband having an affair? No, he wasn't. When she finally confronted him directly, he explained that he had been facing a major challenge at work which had been preoccupying him, as well as a sudden offer of a promotion which would entail a move from the UK to Africa. He had been mulling it over anxiously before mentioning it to her as he knew that her mother was in a nursing home with dementia and that she was also worried about her father, who had recently had a stroke.

* * * * * * *

Managers in particular are often deterred from recognizing and using their own intuitive powers because they feel that somehow, intuition is not scientific enough. The cult of the rational manager has an iron grip on such minds. But this is nonsense. Some of the most celebrated scientists have been intuitive in their work. Albert Einstein speaks with some authority on the point:

> There is no logical way to the discovery of these elemental laws. There is only the way of intuition, which is helped by a feeling for the order lying behind the appearance.

Therefore, encourage intuition in yourself. Become more aware of it. Be more receptive to its often faint whisper. It is potentially a good guide in difficult circumstances.

* * * * * * *

Our minds may indeed be the wonder of the universe but they are also containers of its deepest mysteries. Therefore, we shall never quite know what constitutes the art of judgment. As President John F. Kennedy once said:

> The essence of ultimate decision remains impenetrable to the observer – often, indeed, to the decider himself... There will always be the dark and tangled stretches in the decision-making process – mysterious even to those who may be most intimately involved.

Key points: Experience – the seedbed

- The functions of the conscious mind – *analysing*, *synthesizing* and *valuing* – can also take place on a deeper subconscious level;

- Your subconscious mind embraces much of your memory and is the seat of your values. It is also a workshop where creative synthesis takes place;

- One of the other residents of your depth mind is your conscience – that useful faculty which taps you on the shoulder when you are tempted to stray from your path;

- Intuition is the power or faculty of immediately apprehending that something is the case. It seems to occur without any conscious reasoning;

- We can all remember what Shakespeare once called 'Salad days, when I was green in judgment'. Time and life are our teachers: judgment grows under the hedgerows of experience;

- There is plenty of evidence that effective decision-makers do listen to their intuition. Those who work against the grain of their mind may find they get splinters in their hands;

- Where strong emotions are in play, intuition can be highly unreliable. Equally, physical states such as tiredness or stress can distort the mind's natural workings. It is the whole person who thinks, not just the mind;

- Instinct, flair and intuition are cut from the same cloth. Flair is an instinctive power of discernment in a certain field. You can 'smell' an opportunity or the direction of the path to success;

- At its best intuition works because more information is going into your mind through your senses than your faculties at their conscious level can process so your subconscious mind does some informal analysing, synthesizing and valuing, and an intuition that occurs in the conscious mind is one of its flowers. Experience is the seedbed of judgment;

- If an intuition comes to you after a longish period of time, it is likely to be more reliable; if it comes very early in the story, take your time in checking it out.

> *... there is a dark*
> *Inscrutable workmanship that reconciles*
> *Discordant elements, makes them cling together*
> *In one society*

WILLIAM WORDSWORTH, *THE PRELUDE*

4

Truth – the leading star

Seek the truth: it always shows us
What we should do,
What we should not do,
And what we should stop doing.

LEO TOLSTOY

LA VALLETTE, THE 72-YEAR-OLD Grand Master of the Knights of St John, commanded Malta during the great siege by an immense force of Turks three centuries ago. Upon hearing the news that there was no hope of an early relief he read this dispatch to his Council: 'We now know,' Vallette said, 'that we must not look to others for our deliverance! It is only upon God and our own swords that we may rely. Yet this is no cause for us to be disheartened. Rather the opposite, for it is *better to know the truth of one's situation than to be deceived by specious hopes.'*

In that last sentence La Vallette supplies us with a good working definition of truth. Truth is always *about* something; reality is that *about which* truth is. You can see that there is a certain circularity in that definition but, as the old Chinese saying goes, *The wing carries the bird, but the bird carries the wings.*

Truth itself – so to speak – is a value, and valuing is not subordinate to the analytic synthetic powers of the mind. You can analyse the facts, but you can't get any value from a fact, or, for that matter, an *ought* from an *is*. Like goodness or beauty, truth itself – so to speak – is a simple, indefinable, unanalysable and non-natural property. But it is still possible for us – to our deep pleasure and enjoyment – to identify certain things or people as pre-eminently good, true or beautiful. A Yemeni proverb captures that kind of response: *A gazelle needs no ornaments to be beautiful.*

Thinking at the abstract level about the reality of values such as truth, beauty or goodness is the province of philosophers. What pays dividends for more down-to-earth practical leaders is to act *as if* truth is real: that is, to act as if it can be observed, sought, discovered, embraced. Truth is also open-ended and inexhaustible.

'Truth is open to everyone,' said Seneca, 'and the claims are not all staked yet.'

The rational grounds for making an act of this kind is given to us by a little-known book by the German philosopher Hans Vaihinger (1852–1933). In *The Philosophy of As If*, Vaihinger explores in some depth what he calls 'notions which *cannot* stand for realities, but can be treated *as if* they did, because to do so leads to practical results'.

His principle example is science, where the *as if* assumption concerning truth has led to discovery after discovery. And science – the quest for truth – is a deeply human activity. As Francis Bacon wrote: 'The inquiry of truth, which is the love-making or wooing of it; the knowledge of truth which is the presence of it; and the belief of truth, which is the enjoying of it, is the sovereign good of human nature.'

Truth in business

It is a mark of the best of business leaders that they set a high store on truth. Like La Vallette in the Siege of Malta long ago, they always seek to know the truth of their ever-changing situation. You will find no better model of such a business leader than Lord Roy Thomson, of whom a senior colleague said:

His most memorable quality was his instinctive habit of telling the truth. His strength, which was very great, particularly in dark moments, made him enjoy truth when another man would have found illusion more comfortable. He always faced reality and he always believed that he would do good business in terms of the reality that he faced.

These associated habits of seeking and speaking the truth have one incalculable benefit in human relations, one that far outweighs all the mental effort required to see reality, and the oral courage sometimes needed if you are going to respond to it with the appropriate action, for there is a golden principle in human affairs:

Truth begets trust. And trust is the bedrock of all personal relations, professional or private.

In this respect, a latter-day Roy Thomson is Sir Terry Leahy. He joined Tesco when he was 23, and later became the company's first marketing director before reaching the apex as chief executive officer.

As CEO of Tesco, Sir Terry transformed the company's fortunes, turning it into the UK's largest retailer, employing over 500,000 people worldwide. In *Management in Ten Words* (2012), Leahy draws on a lifetime's experience to show how any manager in any organization can achieve extraordinary results by following ten simple principles and top of the list he puts the principle of truth.

IF I HAD TO CHOOSE which of the ten words is the most important, I would say it is truth. Getting to the truth about the cause of a problem, and then not hiding it; the truthful answer to the question 'what is the purpose of this organization?'; being true to oneself and those around you: seeking and speaking the truth is not merely morally right, but is the bedrock of successful management. And often it is those you serve, your customers, who are the source of the truth. Listen and learn from them, heed their advice however difficult it may be, and you stand a greater chance of success. It's that simple.

During the Second World War the Nazi government in Germany tried to make propaganda a new weapon of war. In England, however, the Ministry of Information realized that if people thought they were fighting for a more democratic future, this had to be reflected in how news about the war was presented. In other words, it had to be fundamentally different from the kind of practices of the dictatorships of Nazi Germany and later Soviet Russia that shaped George Orwell's vision of a Ministry of Truth operating in a totalitarian state, with the aim of subordinating every aspect of life to the omnipresent rule of 'Big Brother', the State.

Research into the 'home intelligence' archive of the Ministry of Information reveals that people at the time were saying insistently, loud and clear, that 'We want the truth, even if it's bad. We want to be treated as adults. Don't patronize us, don't treat us as children. We'll feel much better if we know where we stand.'

Following Winston Churchill's fine example in this respect, the Ministry of Information acted accordingly. Why? Because, as the chief researcher writes, 'There was a clear feeling that we were fighting the war for freedom, democracy and the truth – and those things were indivisible.'

Do your political leaders act on the same principle?

The unwillingness of those in the highest positions in business to seek truth – to face the realities of their situations and to lead with courage – is not just a child of our turbulent times. The historian Thucydides commented thus on the prevalence of misjudgments and their dire consequences: 'So little trouble do men take in the search after truth,' he wrote, 'so readily do they accept whatever comes first to hand.' For the Ancient Greeks, crowding into their theatres, Greek tragedy served as a mirror of all their misjudgments and their dire consequences.

One unerring mark of the love of truth is not entertaining any propositions with greater assurance than the proofs it is built upon will warrant.

JOHN LOCKE, ENGLISH PHILOSOPHER AND PHYSICIAN (1637–1704)

Key points: Truth – the leading star

- Establishing the truth – the realities of the situation or what is in fact the case – is always a necessary condition for effective decision-making. Not that it is easy. Indeed, in some situations the truth may be hard to come by yet truth, however disenchanting, is better than falsehood, however comforting;

- 'Would that I could discover truth as I can uncover falsehood,' said Cicero. It is always easier to know what is *not* true than to know what is true. Therefore truth, like gold, is not always to be obtained – so to speak – but sometimes met by washing away from it all that is not gold;

- As an Arabic proverb says, *Truth is the salt of mankind.* For truth begets trust, and trust is indeed the essential flavour and preservative in all enduring personal relations. Truth is the meaning of reality;

- Nobody knows what truth is, and yet, as Pascal says, 'We have an idea of truth, invincible to all scepticism.' But to act *as if* truth exists and can be explored and mapped is a key belief underlying the great adventure of Science. Einstein exemplified both this belief and the attitude stemming from it;

- For a good business leader truth is not just what might be called factual accuracy – reflecting reality – although that remains important. It also signifies trustworthiness, reliability and straightforwardness;

- For these reasons Sir Terence Leahy believes that 'unearthing the truth is the foundation of good management'. 'Having the courage to act on the truth,' he adds, 'turns a manager into a leader. And in challenging times, we need that courage more than ever.'

- In every business there are certain principles that have a core of truth established over long periods of time. Take Winston Churchill's advice and seek 'to take wide and general views, and to search resolutely and anxiously amid the incidents of business for the dominant truths'.

If we could first know where we are, and whither we are tending, we could better judge what to do, and how to do it.

ABRAHAM LINCOLN

5

Clear thinking

Clear thinking may not succeed in arriving at the truth; but the truth cannot be arrived at without clear thinking.

R.W. JEPSON

TO BE CLEAR is to be free of all impediments in your vision. In the physical context, such impediments include clouds, mist, fog, haze, muddiness, dullness or dimness. In the more figurative sense, it means that you are unambiguous, not confused or doubtful, vague or fuzzy. What is clear is easily understood; it is neither obscure nor indistinct.

Just how we pass from the state of mind of being 'in the dark' about something to being 'in the clear' or 'seeing it in daylight' is often imperceptible. 'I keep the subject constantly before me,' a scientist once remarked to me, 'and wait till the first dawnings open slowly, by little and little, into full and clear light.'

> *The two limits of every unit of thinking are a perplexed,*
> *troubled, or confused situation at the beginning, and a*
> *cleared-up, unified, resolved situation at the close.*

JOHN DEWEY

Positive waiting of this kind, with one's attention wide open and ready, is simply giving your subconscious time to do its work. You are mindful of the problem but trustful of your mind. It is something you often first learn in the schoolroom.

POSITIVE WAITING

THERE IS A WAY OF giving our attention to the data of a problem in geometry without trying to find the solution, or to the words of a Latin or Greek text without trying to arrive at the meaning, a way of waiting, when we are writing, for the right word to come of itself at the end of our pen, while we merely reject all inadequate words.

All wrong translations, all absurdities in geometry problems, all clumsiness of style and all faulty connection of ideas in compositions and essays, all such things are due to the fact that thought has seized upon some idea too hastily and being thus prematurely blocked is not open to the truth. The cause is always that we have wanted to be too active; we have wanted to carry out a search.

SIMONE WEIL, *WAITING FOR GOD* (1949)

'Clear thinking,' said Professor Dorothy Emmet, 'is rather of the nature of an acquired skill which comes through long practice.'

My own belief is that it should start in the home and at school – university is too late.

Reasoning

Reason usually implies the need of justification – either to oneself or another – of some practice, action, opinion or belief; it is usually personal in its reference; thus, a father asks the *reason* for his son's disobedience; a person gives *reasons* for their preference.

Reason is often applied to a motive, consideration, or inducement which one offers in explanation or defence.

BEWARE OF RATIONALIZATION

BECAUSE WE ARE RATIONAL BEINGS we are often tempted to rationalize: to offer or subconsciously adopt a plausible but specious explanation of one's behaviour or attitude.

American statesman, inventor and scientist Benjamin Franklin (1706–90) captured this tendency in a nutshell: 'so convenient a thing is it to be a reasonable creature, since it enables one to find or make a reason for everything one had a mind to do.'

Ground is often used in place of *reason* because it too implies the intent to justify or defend. When, however, the emphasis is on evidence, data, facts or logical reasoning rather than on motives or considerations, *ground* is the acceptable word. Thus, the *reasons* for a belief may explain why it is held, but the grounds for it give evidence of the validity of the belief. *Ground* also suggests more solid support in fact and therefore greater cogency and objectivity than *reason*, thus one may speak of frivolous or trumped-up *reasons* but not *grounds*.

Although *argument* descends from the Latin verb *arguere* (to make clear), it stresses the intent to convince another or others, or to bring them into agreement with one's view or position. It can imply the use of evidence and reasoning in the making and stating of a point in support of one's contention, but often it suggests reasoning without reference to fact – such as an appeal to the emotions. Thus, an *argument* may be no more than an exchange of views, especially an angry or passionate one.

Reasoning before action

'Rightly to be great is not to stir without great argument,' wrote Shakespeare. Clearly, he uses 'argument' here in the classical sense of making something clear. Therefore by 'great argument', Shakespeare meant a debate of high quality upon the reasons for and against the various courses of action.

We owe this concept of argument to the Greeks. Thucydides put into the mouth of the most famous Athenian statesman Pericles these words:

The great impediment of action is in our opinion not discussion but the want of that knowledge which is gained by discussion prior to action. For we have a peculiar power of thinking before we act too, whereas other men are courageous from ignorance but hesitate upon reflection.

XERXES – THE KING WHO DID NOT LISTEN

XERXES, KING OF THE VAST Persian domains, ruled as an autocrat. After his father's failure to conquer Greece, he summoned his nobles and generals to advise him about one further attempt. Actually, he had already made up his mind to do so.

At the General Council his courtiers flattered his judgment, one after another, in what was clearly a charade. Only his uncle Artanabus, an experienced general, had the courage to speak truth to his face:

King, if conflicting opinions are not voiced, it is impossible in making a choice to select the better: one must put into play what has been spoken. If they are voiced, it is possible to choose the better. In like manner we do not discern pure gold by itself but when we rub it against other gold, we determine the better.

Predictably, Xerxes turned his face away.

An immense Persian army crossed the Hellespont on a bridge of boats, won some small initial victories, but then suffered two major catastrophic defeats on sea and land.

What became of Xerxes? He was assassinated.

Argument of the best quality is usually conducted by rational men and women who wish to become clear about what they should or do believe. They may be partly clear but not wholly so, or they may not be completely convinced. They want to hear other points of view. They are in principle willing to change and accept those other points of view if they are more coherent and supported by the weight of evidence. They will entertain any opinion or adopt any of the proposed courses of action as long as reason – the balance of consequences judged in the light of the common purpose – emerges from the argument to favour it.

Clarity – but not necessarily precision

Clarity – as a necessary condition in the search for truth – should not be confused with precision. You can be clear about a concept – for example, friendship – without being able to define it precisely. Here, common sense will seldom lead one so far astray. As Aristotle observed: 'It is a mark of the educated man and a proof of his culture that in every subject he looks for only so much precision as its nature permits.'

* * * * * * *

An example of clear thinking

This example of clear thinking distinguishes between *purpose, aims, objectives* and *steps* and explores their relationships. It is like that fabulous ladder in Jacob's dream in Genesis (28:12), stretching from heaven to earth, with angels descending and ascending.

You can now see that descending the Jacob's ladder, from the general and abstract to the particular and concrete, you are answering the question 'How?' This is my *purpose*. Yes, but *how* are you going to achieve it? By tackling these *aims* or *goals*.

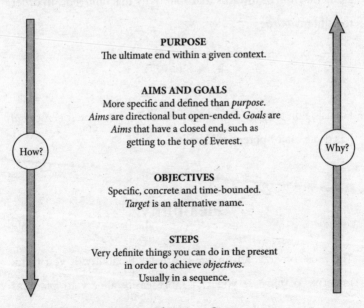

PURPOSE
The ultimate end within a given context.

AIMS AND GOALS
More specific and defined than *purpose*.
Aims are directional but open-ended. *Goals* are
Aims that have a closed end, such as
getting to the top of Everest.

How?

Why?

OBJECTIVES
Specific, concrete and time-bounded.
Target is an alternative name.

STEPS
Very definite things you can do in the present
in order to achieve *objectives*.
Usually in a sequence.

Figure 5.1 *Purpose, Aims, Objectives, Steps*

Notice that *aims* are really no more than *purpose* broken down into manageable parts. It is like light being refracted into the colours of the rainbow. The same is true of the next stage in the descent. Take any one *aim*, how are you going to achieve it? Answer: by achieving these *objectives*. Now pick out any of these *objectives*: how are you going to accomplish that? Answer: by taking these *steps*. Today? Yes, there's bound to be one of those *steps* that you can take right now!

Going upwards rather than downwards, you are then answering the '*why?*' question. Why are you taking this *step*? In order to achieve this *objective*. Why this *objective*? To move along that *aim* or towards that *goal*. Why that *aim/goal*? In order to fulfil my *purpose*.

* * * * * * *

Focusing on *purpose* and *aims* rather than upon one specific *goal* has three major potential benefits.

Flexibility

The most obvious advantage is greater flexibility. If you think in terms of *purpose* you can more easily alter your plans as circumstances arise. On the other hand, if you lock yourself into a *goal* like an intercontinental missile, then you are much more likely to be shot down and lose all.

In times of change you do have to be more general in your intention in order to give yourself maximum leeway – the allowable margin of freedom or variation. Remember, Christopher Columbus was sailing for India when he discovered America. Because his purpose was to *explore*? Be that as it may, we do not regard him as a failure.

A sense of direction

A *purpose* in life, especially when refracted into more definite aims, may well develop in you a sense of overall direction. It serves like the Pole Star in the sky in that respect. You will never reach the star itself, but it can guide you to your destination.

By another analogy, your purpose should act like a magnetic force that draws you in a certain direction. You may make navigational errors, but that magnetic influence – that vector – constantly affects the compass of your spirit and if you heed it, draws you back on course. 'Our plans miscarry because they have no aim,' wrote Seneca. 'When a man does not know what harbour he is making for, no wind is the right wind.'

A measure of progress

From time to time, you may want to appraise yourself in terms of progress. If you think in terms of a specific objective or goal, it is relatively easy to know if you succeed or fail. I mean, either you did become President of the United States or you did not. And with goals like that, there is plenty of scope for failure. As Epictetus wrote: 'One must not tie a ship to a single anchor, nor life to a single hope.'

If, on the other hand, you are focused on *purpose*, it follows that you will find it harder to experience total success or failure – only a series of successes or failures. The latter may in reality be indicators of progress, but they are imperfect measuring instruments and you will need to develop a more holistic judgment. We should seek to measure what we value, not value what we can easily measure in quantifiable ways.

AN EXERCISE IN CLEAR THINKING

IN ONE SENTENCE, WRITE DOWN the *purpose* or vision of your life as a whole.

Now, write down two or three *aims* which make that purpose a bit more concrete or tangible.

Remember, aims tend to be long-term and directional. They can be either open (*aims*) or closed (*goals*).

So, that's the easy bit done!

The French painter Claude Monet (1840–1926) once declared that his purpose in life was to dispel each day some of the fog that surrounds us. Art – or at least in the hands of a master like Leonardo da Vinci – is a form of clear thinking.

Fog surrounds us and sometimes invades us, both in our professional and personal lives. But there is a remedy: clear thinking. It's a blade that you should keep sharp even though it lives for most of the time in a sheath ready for use.

Key points: Clear thinking

- Some problems become clearer if you wait for dregs or impurities to sink to the bottom of the water. Quiet and patient attention feeds your purposive subconscious;

- Thoughts that 'lie too deep for words' cannot be put to serious or practical use. Those who claim to reach conclusions by way of them are often merely admitting that they have shirked the effort without which ideas cannot be clarified;

- Clear expression and clear thinking are complementary and there are no shortcuts to either;

- Reasoning with others to make things clear before action makes good sense. As the Chinese proverb says: *When*

*the lamp is trimmed by discussion, the truth shines
more brightly.*

- 'All men have a reason, but not all men can give a reason.'
  In argument, the clever, articulate person always has an
  advantage. But a wise person will sense when they are
  talking to someone who has a reason but has difficulty in
  putting it into words;

- As a leader you need to be able to generate and lead
  the kind of discussion that creates informed decisions.
  Remember, too, the great principle that the more people
  share in making decisions that affect their working lives,
  the more they are committed to carrying them out;

- The language of truth is simple.

*Derive happiness in oneself from a good day's work,
from illuminating the fog that surrounds us.*
HENRI MATISSE

PART TWO

LEADING WITH JUDGMENT

6

Your first vocation

From the gods comes the saying: 'Know yourself'.
JUVENAL, *SATIRES* (SECOND CENTURY)

THE ART OF JUDGMENT, like charity, begins at home. You need to exercise it in your choice of occupation or career, and – usually later – of life partner, customarily your husband or wife. In the making of those personal choices, there is much to be learnt – sometimes the hard way – about the nature and practice of good judgment in general.

What is vocation?

In the English language today *vocation* is one of a set of words – *occupation, career, profession, trade* – that apply to the kind of work we do to earn our living. *Vocation* is based upon the Latin *vocare* to call; its closest synonym in English is *calling*.

In the ancient Hebrew language, just as in modern English, to *call* someone is to summon them loudly. Of all those ancient prophets said to have been called by God, notice that not one of them claimed they didn't hear and none of them refused.

This fact is indicative: it takes us back to Genesis, where you may remember that God *calls* everything into existence, one by one – including ultimately Adam and Eve, our mythical ancestors. It's a creative act. Therefore, the best way to think about vocation is in terms of creation – it's what or who you are.

As human beings we are distinct from other living creatures in that three strands go into our making: we are *individual embodied persons*. Our *embodiment* in male or female forms is something we do share with our evolutionary cousins, and for much the same purpose. But the two other elements in the equation mean that you are both unique – utterly unlike anyone else – as an *individual*; while, at the same time, you are like everyone else in being a *person* – a concept that transcends sex or gender, age, colour, race or creed.

It is the creational fact of our individuality which makes us more suitable for a certain kind of work rather than for others. Plato in *The Republic* was the first author in history to draw attention to this critically important fact.

THE PRINCIPLE OF VOCATION

'NOR NEED THAT SURPRISE US,' I rejoined. 'For as you were speaking, it occurred to me that, in the first place, no two of us are born exactly alike. We have different natural aptitudes which fit us for different jobs.'

'We have indeed.'

'So do we do better to exercise one skill or to try to practise several?'

'To stick to one,' he said.

'And there is a further point. It is fatal in any job to miss the right moment for action.'

'Clearly.'

'The workman must be a professional at the call of his job; his job will not wait till he has leisure to spare for it.'

'That is inevitable.'

'Quantity and quality are therefore more easily produced when a man specializes appropriately on a single job for which he is naturally fitted, and neglects all others.'

'That's certainly true.'

PLATO, *THE REPUBLIC* (381 BC)

The Law of Variety – the fact that we are all different – means that some people will know at a very young age what they want to do. For example, Raymond Briggs, author of the classic children's book and film *The Snowman* (which has no words), knew at the age of five or six that he wanted to be a cartoonist. Can you think of other examples? On the other hand, others will have a long journey ahead of them before they discover their vocation in life. And some never do.

Three key factors in choosing your work

For many of us, the main problem is at the time when pressed to make a decision, we just do not know ourselves – or the realities of the world for that matter – to enable us to make an informed choice. But it's not a new problem. Back in the eighteenth century, Dr Samuel Johnson observed:

> Why, sir, the greatest concern we have in this world, the choice of our profession, must be determined without demonstrative reasoning. Human life is not yet so well known, as that we can have it.

It helps to focus your attention on three key questions:

| *What are your interests?* | An interest is a state of feeling in which you wish to pay particular attention to something. Longstanding interests – those you naturally like – make it much easier to acquire knowledge and skills. |

| *What are your aptitudes?* | Aptitudes are your natural abilities, what you are fitted for by disposition. An aptitude is a capacity that may range from being a gift or talent to simply being above average. |
| *What are the relevant factors in your temperament?* | Temperament is an important factor. Some people, for example, are uncomfortable in decision-making situations of stress and danger, while others thrive on them. |

Aptitudes

Just as a reminder, your *aptitudes* are your natural abilities, what you are fitted for by disposition. In particular, an *aptitude* signifies *your capacity to learn or acquire a particular skill*. For example, supposing your aptitudes for music, languages and maths are very low. That doesn't mean you cannot enjoy singing in the bath, or embarrassing your companion by speaking in French in Calais, or doing your own accounts. But these activities should not form a substantial part of your professional work.

Aptitude, you recall, can usefully be distinguished from *skill*, which suggests both some form of learned knowledge and the ability to use that knowledge effectively and readily in execution or performance. This learned power of doing something competently only develops – or is developed – over a period of time.

There are various ways of categorizing aptitudes – mechanical, linguistic, artistic, musical and so on. No one scheme of classifying them is to be preferred to another. Anyway, not all aptitudes can be classified or put into pigeonholes in such a neat way. Having an aptitude obviously implies the likelihood of success in it, for you are working with the grain of the wood, not against it. As I have said earlier, the natural level of motivation balances the aptitude. Your *interest* will be engaged. In *The Taming of the Shrew* (Act I, Scene I), Shakespeare says:

> No profit grows where no pleasure ta'en;
> In brief, sir, study what you most affect [love].

Interests

Interests are also natural endowments. Moreover, they are extremely important clues in your personal quest to find your vocation.

Interest has been defined as a state of feeling in which you wish to pay particular attention to something. You might have an interest in, for example, old coins or military history or the ballet. They may not be labelled 'interests' in your mind, they may even fall below the status of a conscious interest, but those feelings divert you to look outwards at something beyond yourself.

The idea that our interests are part of our talent is not a familiar one. *Talent* originates from the Greek *talanton*, a balance for weighing precious metals. A natural disposition or interest is like an inclination of the scales. Your mind – or as Shakespeare said, 'what you most affect' – tilts one way rather than another, as if responding to a magnetic attraction. Hence my idea that an interest can be categorized as a form of talent.

Exercise

Make a list of your *three* principal interests, those which naturally draw your attention and upon which you have spent time and money.

Put a star by any which has lasted more than five years. Put two stars if the interest manifested itself before you were 18 years old.

It's sometimes easier to know what doesn't interest you rather than what does, so now list three occupations for which you have zero interest.

The interests which are the gold and silver of vocation tend to be ones which manifest themselves in childhood or early in life, long before you have considered what career you will pursue. As Graham Greene wrote in *The Power and the Glory* (1940),

'There is always one moment in childhood when the door opens and lets the future in.' Be that as it may, perceptive parents may sometimes discern the seeds of the future in the present interests and activities of their children.

Temperament

I'm tempted to call this *personality*, but personality could be taken to include aptitudes and interests, and I want to differentiate this third area a little more clearly. Most of us like to see ourselves in a good light, and that desire may blind us to the realities of our temperament so we sometimes launch into careers for which – it appears later – we are not temperamentally suited.

Temperament, then, is obviously an integral part of your make-up and it is the most difficult aspect of yourself to change. As a common-sense general principle it is best to work within the compass of your temperament – which is not to say that you shouldn't try to control its less helpful elements! For when it comes to temperament it's important to remember that it's all about *tendencies*. To describe someone as temperamentally lazy only means that he or she has a *tendency* to be lazy. To be quick-tempered or aggressive doesn't mean to say that you always lose your temper or seem to attack people. Therefore, you should always be cautious about using your temperament as an excuse for not doing what you should or shouldn't do. When her son told the author Dorothy L. Sayers that he was temporarily separated from his wife, blaming his explosive temperament, she replied with a long letter of rebuke:

> I know all about 'temperament'; it is the word we use for our own egotism, and, for our own bad temper and bad manners – and the mere fact that we use the word implies that we intend to take no serious trouble to control ourselves... Let me hear that you have made it up with Jeanne, for whom I have every sympathy.

CHECKLIST – SOME TEMPERAMENTAL FACTORS

- Do you prefer working with others rather than on your own?
- Would you rather lead a team than take instructions?
- Would you describe yourself more as at the introvert than the extrovert end of the spectrum?
- Or are you somewhere in the middle ground – an ambivert?
- Would you describe yourself as very cautious and risk-averse?
- Can you work in a stressful environment?
- Do you work best with the pressure of deadlines?
- What are the five adjectives most commonly used by others who know you well to describe your temperament?
- Do you prefer to work more outdoors or more indoors?
- Are you happy to do repetitive work or routine administration?

- How important is variety and challenge to you?
- Is the prospect of promotion to higher responsibility essential for you?
- Are you naturally competitive?
- In what ways does your present job, if you have one, not suit your temperament?

Not that I'm assuming you will have a perfect picture of these three factors. How people acquire knowledge of themselves would take a book in itself. What matters is to acquire *working* self-knowledge in relation to work. It often starts from a very early age as a child begins to explore its environment.

Being social beings by nature, we humans both give and receive observations and comments on others. Patterns begin to take shape in this informal or formal feedback (for example, in school reports), and some general ideas gradually coalesce. We discover what we are and are not so good at, what we like most and what we like less. Our natural profile of aptitudes, interests and temperament slowly emerges, to be tested and modified over time.

Identifying the feasible options

Having achieved a working knowledge of your aptitudes, interests and temperament – the solicited or unsolicited comments of others who know you can be immensely helpful here – the next step is to list your options. Here, the Lobster Pot Model from Chapter Two (*reproduced here*) can be useful.

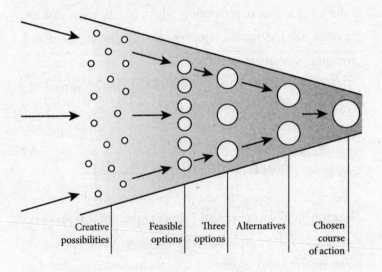

| Creative possibilities | Feasible options | Three options | Alternatives | Chosen course of action |

As the Lobster Pot Model shows, you need to open your mind into wide focus to consider all possibilities, and that is where creative thinking comes in. But then your valuing faculty must come into play in order to identify the feasible options. *Feasible* means capable of being done or carried out or realized. If an option is feasible, it has some real likelihood of being workable. It can attain the end you have in mind.

In the vocational context the feasible options are the ones accessible to you *now* or in the near future in terms of age and paper qualification requirements. Equally important, these occupations hold out the promise that they will engage your natural interests and employ your natural aptitudes, so you might well expect to be successful in that respect too. I'm not thinking in the first instance of promotion, which is a separate issue. On the other hand, if you are temperamentally strongly ambitious, promotional prospects are something to take into account.

Having now made a list of your *feasible* options, the next step is to eliminate the less attractive ones.

Narrowing down the list

The eminent philosopher Karl Popper points out that in science it is virtually impossible to *verify* anything; what you can do, however, is to *falsify* proportions. In vocational choice situations the same is true. It is usually easier to establish that one course or career is *not* suitable or is unlikely to be successful in terms of your vocational aim than to discover what is the right one.

How can this process of elimination be carried out? What you need to do is to *gather more information*. Here are some possibilities for doing so:

- *Using your imagination.* Removing your 'rose-tinted spectacles', picture yourself in the characteristic working situations of the profession or trade you have in mind.

Obviously the more you know about that occupation, the more realistic this self-projection will be. Beware of wanting to *be* something – a politician, for example – but not to *do* the work. Still interested?

- *Ask a practitioner or two.* Informally 'interviewing' a few people already engaged in that job is usually revealing. Do so in their place of work if possible. Remember, however, to *choose vocational people*, those who love their work. Compared to the others, you will actually find them *more* truthful about the realities of the work. They will tell you where the shoe pinches. Are they the sort of people you can naturally accept as 'role models'? Do you feel really put off by what they say?

- *Have a trial.* Sometimes you can test a precarious-looking footbridge without committing yourself to cross it. If time and circumstances allow, try to get some experience of the work and see what it is like. As the old military proverb affirms, *time spent on reconnaissance is seldom wasted.*

You have now only two or three feasible options left on the list. As you have sieved out the less value-laden ones, for one good vocational reason or another, those you are left with may present you with a difficult choice. How do you decide?

Usually the trick is to go on accumulating and piling *information* about the two (or three) options into the scale-pans, and gradually you will find that one side moves down. The decision, if you like, is making itself. It is as if you flow in one direction and not in the other, and – noticing this direction – you say to yourself, 'I have decided.'

If you are really stuck, sleep on it – allow your subconscious mind to do its work.

THE WISDOM OF SIGMUND FREUD

IN A PSYCHOANALYTIC SESSION THE other day, I controlled the impulse to remark, 'When I was five and twenty, I heard a wise old man say'… A young man had come to consult me about two decisions that he had to make: should he follow a certain profession and ought he to marry a certain girl? Something in him or in his situation reminded me of myself at his age. He had just received his doctorate in psychology. I, too, had won my PhD at this age and I was a student of Freud.

One evening I ran into the great man on his daily walk along the Ringstrasse in Vienna, and walked home with him. Friendly as always, he asked me about my plans and I told him of my problems, which resembled those of my present patient. Of course, I hoped Freud would give me advice or resolve my doubts.

'I can only tell you of my personal experience,' he said. 'When making a decision of minor importance, I have always found it advantageous to consider all the pros and cons. In vital matters, however, such as the choice of a mate or a profession, the decision should come from the unconscious, from somewhere within ourselves. In the important decisions of our personal life, we should be governed, I think, by the deep inner needs of our nature.'

Without telling me what to do, Freud had helped me make my own decision. Like marriage, the choice of a profession is a matter of destiny. We should welcome our destiny, readily accepting what comes with and out of it. On that evening thirty-five years ago when I decided to become a psychoanalyst, I married the profession for better or for worse.

DR THEODOR REIK, *LISTENING WITH THE THIRD EAR* (1948)

Other people – parents, relatives, teachers, friends, superiors – may have strong views about what you should do with your life. Listen to what they say, even if it is unsolicited advice, for they know you (in part, perhaps) and the world – or at least some of it. But the responsibility is yours alone for answering the vocational question: 'What shall I do with my life?'

If subtle pressure builds up and other forms of opposition develop, stay calm and quietly determined to follow your own inner compass. You may get lost, but it will be *your* lostness: you don't want to live with the shadow of what-might-have-been.

Remember, vocational people are tenacious when facing difficulties. You are bound to face discouragement at some stage or other, although the worst is what comes from those dear to you. Yet it is vocation that sets your feet on the adventure of your life, and you cannot miss out on that. '*If you look behind you,*' says a proverb of the Australian Aborigines, '*you will never leave.*'

From trial-and-error to trial and improve

Trial-and-error is a method of finding out the best way to reach a desired result or a correct solution by trying out one or more ways or means and noting and eliminating errors or courses of failure. More loosely, it means the trying of this and that until something succeeds.

When applied to finding your vocation, this strategy has the drawback that it is very time-consuming. On the other hand, the experience gained in the 'false starts' can be put to use – a theme I shall explore in the next chapter.

You cannot avoid experience – actually testing it out by doing it – in your quest for vocation. There is no such thing as armchair vocation. The aim of this chapter is to ensure that you do not expend too much time in fields where you are a misfit. I speak from experience – it's easily done! Using these techniques, you should be able to make an intelligent choice of a 'front runner'. That's not to say it's right for you. At least you will be more or less in the right field. But remember, it's still a *hypothesis*. Your vocation may well be in that direction, but until you have tried it, you will not know for sure.

If you adopt this experimental approach, even after you have made your decision and initially committed yourself, your subconscious mind will soon give you signs if you are on the wrong course.

Beware of giving up too easily – all vocations are daunting in their early stages. But if it's not for you, stay calm and polite, but firmly part company. Cut your losses. You haven't failed, you have just eliminated one possibility.

Before Thomas Edison (1847–1931) achieved success in inventing the light bulb, a newspaper reporter asked him, 'Why do you persist in spending all this time and money when you have failed so many times?'

'Young man,' Edison replied, 'you don't understand how this world works! I have not failed. I have successfully discovered over 100 ways that do not work. That puts me over 100 ways closer to the way which does!'

Are you condemned to frustration? Not necessarily. Take a fresh look at your present situation and see what vocational possibilities, if any, it holds for you. You may not see them at once, but they may emerge after a time of reflection. Sometimes vocational people seem to transform their present situations in a creative and innovative way, even though these situations are not of their own choosing and are far from what the world might call favourable or promising.

Crossing the Rubicon

In the big judgments of your life your degree of commitment is always a success factor. Wholehearted implementation of a less-than-perfect plan pays more dividends than half-hearted dawdling on the perfect plan. The whole purpose of judgment is that you stand wholehearted and free of doubt at the altar.

In 49 BCE, declaring '*Jacta alea esto*, Let the dice be cast!', Julius Caesar crossed the River Rubicon, the boundary between Cisalpine Gaul and Rome's own territory, thereby committing himself irrevocably to a bid for supreme power. Casting the dice or crossing the Rubicon are metaphors for such an act of decision. If it is not to be a reckless one, it has to be preceded by a careful act of judgment.

Incidentally, it is actually not easy to know if and when you have committed yourself in the momentous sense. You may have had the experience of committing yourself to, say, giving up smoking or going on a diet, only to find yourself accepting a cigarette or eating far too much of those foods you had shunned for ever! In *The Princess and the Goblin*, George MacDonald describes that very experience:

> He jumped up, as he thought, and began to dress, but, to his dismay, found that he was still in bed. 'Now then I will!' he said, 'Here goes! I *am* up now!' But yet again he found himself snug in bed. Twenty times he tried, and twenty times he failed: for in fact he was not awake, only dreaming that he was.

Sometimes you only know the difference between those 20 dreamy false starts and the twenty-first time, when Rubicon – the point of no return – was *really* crossed, some years later, when you reflect upon your life with the benefit of hindsight. The turning point, the hinge upon which your life swung, will be clear, for your mind will always return to that time and place like a homing pigeon.

Again, usually by hindsight, it looks as if that elusive *sufficient condition* has now been met. The dice you have cast on the table have been met by an answering throw. Something decisive has happened. Things will never be quite the same. You now have a sense of purpose in life; you are on the move, with a new sense of your worth and destiny as a unique person. In his book *Mount Everest Expedition* (1951), W.H. Murray wrote:

> Until one is committed there is hesitancy, the chance to draw back, always ineffectiveness. Concerning all acts of initiative (and creation), there is one elementary truth, the ignorance of which kills the countless ideas and splendid plans: that the moment one definitely commits oneself, then Providence moves too. All sorts of things occur to help one that would never otherwise have occurred. A whole stream of events issues from the decision, raising on one's favour all manner of unforeseen incidents and meetings and material assistance which no man could have dreamt would have come his way. I have learned a deep respect for one of Goethe's couplets: 'Whatever you can do, or dream you can, begin it. Boldness has genius power, and magic in it.'

'Then Providence moves to'... That sense that something *other* has, as it were, accepted your offer and has underwritten your enterprise invites religious language. It is not a specifically Christian experience – Socrates, for example, believed that God had called him to be a philosopher. It is as if the sufficient condition has been fulfilled. Whatever name we give it – Zeus or God, Power or Being – it is on your side. There is sometimes also a sense of assurance, even if the way ahead is clouded in doubt or beset with difficulties. It breeds an inner confidence.

THE CASE OF THE SWEDISH DIPLOMAT

BORN IN 1905, SON OF a Swedish prime minister, Dag Hammarskjöld reached the pinnacle of the world civil service as Secretary General to the United Nations (1954–58). He had to deal with the Suez Crisis (1956) in which he opposed Britain, and his attempts to solve the problem of the Congo (now Zaire) were attacked by the Soviet Union. In pursuit of the solution there, he was killed when his plane crashed, aged 56. He was unmarried.

His private journal of notes and poems, translated by W.H. Auden and published under the title *Markings* (1964), reveals an intensely religious soul but one outside the orbit of any organized religion. A strong sense of dedication is at the centre of his life. It stems from a feeling of relationship with God, a personal call to which he accepted gradually but decisively:

> *I don't know who – or what – put the question,*
> *I don't know when it was put, I don't even remember answering.*

> *But at some moment I did answer Yes to Someone or Something.*
> *And from that hour I was certain that existence is meaningful*
> *And that, therefore, my life, in self-surrender, has a goal.*

The life of Dag Hammarskjöld, both his inner or spiritual life and the course of his career in the world, is enough to scotch the idea that the blessing of a vocation confers any special privileges. The path of demanding service is thorny and uphill, and it may require the acceptance of loneliness and personal self-sacrifice.

CHECKLIST – HAVE YOU MADE THE RIGHT CHOICE?

- Have you a reasonably clear and objective idea of your aptitudes, interests and temperament?

- Are you clear about the callings or professions for which you are *not* well fitted?

- Can you think of another profession, trade or field that you would rather be in?

- Does your present work give you scope for creativity?

- Have you allowed in your work of charting your course for time to 'sleep on it', so as to give your subconscious mind an opportunity to contribute?

- Do you feel that your abilities match the requirements of your particular role or function?

- Do you feel a long-term commitment to your present occupation or field of work?

- Has your enthusiasm for your work been tested and sustained over a period of years?

- Do you have a sense of being, as it were, at the call of your work, and through your work to others?

- In face of difficulties have you shown a power to endure them and to overcome obstacles?

'To create is always to do something new,' said Martin Luther. Vocation is directly or indirectly connected with creativity. Even in traditional occupations or well-established fields vocational people seek new ways of doing things. They are society's agents of change – the change for good we call progress.

Besides creativity the other star in the vocational sky is service. 'I am never weary of being useful,' wrote Leonardo da Vinci. 'In serving others I cannot do enough – no labour is sufficient to tire me.' But you don't have to be a Leonardo to make service to others your end: it is an optional way of interpreting every job, trade or profession. 'No one is useless in this world who lightens the burdens of another,' said Charles Dickens.

In summary, vocation is hard to define but easy to see when it is present in the lives of others. The poet W.H. Auden proposes a simple test:

You need not see what someone is doing
To know if it is his vocation.

You have only to watch his eyes:

A cook making a sauce, a surgeon

Making a primary incision,

A clerk completing a bill of lading,

Wear the same rapt expression,

Forgetting themselves in a function.

The choice of a life partner

Aristotle once defined the two distinctive natural activities of human beings as *building cities* and *coupling*. Most people, not all, have a natural vocation to coupling in general. The call to marry a specific person – the right one, as we say – usually comes later, and often after much trial and error.

To marry X is a decision. Behind all such decisions there is a process of judgment, be it long or short, conscious or subconscious. Like all other stories, in this story there is a kind of generic *beginning*, *middle* and *end*.

- *Beginning*   The two individuals meet. There is a degree of mutual attraction, interest and attention.

  To the initial question: 'Do I want to meet this individual again?', both answer 'yes'.

- *Middle*   A period summed up in a popular song from the musical *The King and I*: 'Getting to know you, getting to know all about you...'

              It is a reciprocal process, for you cannot say that you know someone unless they know you.

              This period may conclude with some form of test or trial, such as going on holiday together.

- *End*   The final stage is the mutual decision to live together, sharing bed and board.

If you turn back to Chapter 1, you may see that there is a family likeness between this simple story-framework in three stages and the process identified there as 'thinking to some purpose' (*see page* 24).

The classic description in English literature of a journey through these three stages is to be found in the novels of Jane Austen, especially *Pride and Prejudice* (1813). Although they are of course fiction – and told from a woman's point of view – they ring true as case studies of the human condition and not just for readers of English literature, for as the French writer Antoine de St Exupéry remarked: 'Truth is the language which identifies the universal.'

One of the difficulties we all face is that we meet possible life partners only one-by-one, in sequence. If someone doesn't feel quite right, do you go ahead and marry them on the grounds (increasing with age) that you will probably not have another chance? It takes courage metaphorically to throw that fish back into the sea. In real life, Jane Austen received only one firm proposal of marriage, from a wealthy but not particularly attractive suitor. She accepted, but then slept on it; the next day she told him that she could not marry him. She received no other proposals, and died in 1817 at the age of 43.

Central to Austen's novels, too, is the difficulty of knowing people. A person's looks and their *personality* are immediately apparent on that first encounter, but *character* cannot be thus known: it reveals itself only over time. You just have to spend time together, ideally in a variety of situations.

Understanding comes from a root meaning 'to stand in the midst of'. It signifies the kind of knowledge of people that comes to you imperceptibly and without your knowing, simply by being with them, or among them, sharing their hardships and difficulties. But it takes time. One English proverb counsels that one should never marry unless one has 'summered and wintered' together.

As Jane Austen's novels show, rational thinking or sound judgment is not the enemy of romantic love, it merely tells you how firm or shaky are the foundations of the proposed life-long relationship. It's the highest example of judgment that most of us encounter in our personal lives. To get it wrong can cause agony. Get it right and it feels (speaking as a man) as if, in Alexander Pope's words:

All other goods by Fortune's hands are given;
A wife is the peculiar gift of heaven.

In most cultures it is the prerogative of the man to propose marriage to the woman, as if he is the one who is doing the choosing. But the reality is usually very different and the choice is a mutual one. C.S. Lewis compared it to two rivulets of rain falling on a window and as they run down, converging towards each other.

So the right time to marry, English proverbial wisdom suggests, is when *both* the man and woman seek each other for life. *It is time to set in, when the oven comes to the dough.* [The implication of this and the next proverb is that the right time to marry is when the woman courts the man.] *It is time to yoke, when the cart comes to the caples* [horses].

Margaret Gane, a young officer in the Women's Royal Air Force in the Second World War, suffered some disappointments and heart-breaking bereavements in her relationships with some of her male contemporaries, but it all changed for her when she met and came to know a Canadian pilot, Squadron Leader George Pushman DFC. In her book, *We All Wore Blue* (2006), she writes of the moment he proposed to her, and recalls how she was

> ...surprised to hear myself saying yes without any hesitation or demurrings. All the doubt, the self-examination, the qualms that had held me back from commitments before, simply did not seem to exist. It was as though everything else in my life had been for the purpose of matching me with this man at this moment.

Not all of us can attain such mutual wholeheartedness in our commitments, but such mutual love – beginning, middle and end – is something we all seek. For our highest need is to love and be loved.

Getting to know people – a holistic process

Bernard Babington Smith, formerly of the Institute of Psychology at Oxford University, has described a useful exercise to illustrate how our knowledge of a group or an individual 'grows' in a holistic way. He describes the model thus:

> The systematic observation of the activities of a group covers what is more easily evident in the observation of a single

individual, 'getting to know' people. Information about a person accumulates, and the question is how best to record, process or employ it.

Thus a model of 'getting to know' people, he continues, may be demonstrated in the following way. Draw in turn, as numbered, the lines of the accompanying diagram and as each is drawn, look at what is drawn and write briefly what is there.

Most people find that at certain stages they see some well-known shape developing, and succeeding lines confirm and support this, but there are stages when they are taken aback by the next addition, and find that the earlier pattern

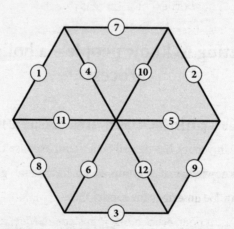

Figure 6.2 *Steps in holistic thinking*

has to be replaced by a new one. (This demonstration will undoubtedly lose by being presented in this way, where the end state can be seen; even so, it may be worth going through the steps or trying it on someone who does not know the final appearance.)

The implication of this model is that we 'get to know' people as 'wholes'. But for some people it seems to make sense to think of others in terms of assessable traits. Theories of personality devised by psychologists may be quite inappropriate for everyday use; it is highly relevant therefore to inquire how people are in fact found to observe and think about others, and inquiry based on the view that traits would be attributed to others on the basis of accumulating and enumerable instances has not borne it out. There is plenty of room for more exploration by observation of the ways in which other people do get to know each other.

Key points: Your first vocation

- Your primary vocation is to be you. What you do at work should be an extension of that. Gerard Manley Hopkins, the Jesuit poet, echoed this in his poem, *Kingfishers and Dragonflies*, 'What I do is me: for that I came.'

- Accept false starts in the search for your vocation. It is all part of the trial-and-error process – learning the hard way!

- It is never unwise to turn back if you are on the wrong road. Don't regard such abandoned courses as failures – see them more as experiments. It all beds down, anyway, in the compost heap of experience;

- Making and implementing a plan always entails taking some *definite steps*, as opposed to just drifting with the stream. Only dead fish do that. But remember the paramount need to balance persistence with flexibility;

- Choose the right partner. Then your vocations in work and family will walk hand-in-hand;

- Out of finding your vocation grows a sense of creative service to others, not only in your field of work, but also in your home and community;

- Is vocation for the few or the many? The door is always open to you to consider your occupation as a vocation. It may require some creative thinking but that prize is there to be won. For I imagine vocation to be like the Caucus-race organized in *Alice in*

Wonderland. At its end, as the Dodo announced after much thought: '*Everybody* has won, and *all* shall have prizes.'

There's a divinity that shapes our ends,
Rough-hew them how we will.
WILLIAM SHAKESPEARE, *HAMLET*, ACT V, SCENE II

7

Leadership – your second vocation

When they call you a reaper, sharpen your scythe.

OLDE ENGLISH PROVERB

YOUR FIRST VOCATION is to be an engineer, soldier, doctor, nurse, teacher or plumber. Your second vocation is as a *leader* of engineers, soldiers, nurses, teachers or plumbers.

Experience in your profession, occupation or trade may result at some point in your career in you being chosen to be a team or first-level leader. But remember, there are thousands of people occupying roles of leadership (because they have domain experience) but who are not actually leaders. For there are thousands of people occupying such positions in enterprises who are not fulfilling the true role of leader.

Role is best understood in terms of the expectations that those involved have of the role-holder. You can be appointed (or elected) a manager or commander but you are not a leader until *your appointment is ratified in the hearts and minds of those who work for you or with you.* That is the fundamental principle of leadership.

In this chapter I offer you some guidelines on how to become a good leader. And remember, as I said earlier, *good is good, better is better.*

LEADERSHIP THAT EVOKES GREATNESS

SIR NEVILLE MARRINER, FOUNDER AND principal conductor of the Academy of St Martin-in-the-Fields, once played in the London Symphony Orchestra:

> As a player, I was with the LSO, which has always been regarded as the second-best orchestra in London. Then Stokowski was persuaded to come and work with the LSO and in about three days he managed to transmit to us the notion that we were a great orchestra. It gave us enormous confidence and we suddenly realised, in one concert at the Festival Hall, that we could achieve, had just achieved, a great performance – that we could achieve it just as easily as any other orchestra in the world. I think it was a great turning point for the orchestra, suddenly to be given this confidence in one performance.

From that moment the LSO never looked back – it was extraordinary. What did he do? He put more responsibility on the players than they had before. He more or less said to them, 'This is your orchestra and if you want it to be good then you must perform. I will do my best to make it happen but the responsibility is yours.' He just had this remarkable ability to focus the emotion of an entire orchestra. His personality was immensely strong.

JAN R. JONASSEN, *LEADERSHIP: SHARING THE PASSION* (1999)

Contrary to popular belief, true leaders do not seek people to be their followers; they are much more intent upon making people feel like *partners* with them in the common enterprise. Fortunately for us, there is no want of great challenges to evoke greatness, creativity and nobility from people. As the tectonic plates of change grind together they throw up hills and mountains of tasks, enough for countless millennia. And so good leaders – and leaders for good – will never want for employment.

'It is provided in the essence of things,' said the American poet, essayist and journalist Walt Whitman, 'that from any fraction of success, no matter what, shall come further something to make a great struggle necessary.'

On leadership

Leadership is often discussed or analysed in terms of leadership qualities. Some of these qualities, such as *intelligence, energy, initiative* and *enthusiasm*, are more universal than others. Leaders tend to (or should) exemplify the qualities expected or required

	QUALITY	FUNCTIONAL VALUE
TASK	*Initiative*	A quality which appears in many research lists. It means the aptitude for initiating or beginning action; the ability to get the group moving.
	Perseverance	The ability to endure; tenacity. Obviously functional in many situations where the group is inclined to give up or is prey to frustrations.
TEAM	*Integrity*	The capacity to integrate; to see the wood for the trees; to bind up parts into a working whole; the attribute that creates a group climate of trust.
	Humour	Invaluable for relieving tension in group or individual, or, for that matter, in the leader themselves. Closely related to a sense of proportion – a useful asset in anything involving people!
INDIVIDUAL	*Tact*	This expresses itself in action by showing sensitive perception of what is fit, or consideration in dealing with others.
	Compassion	Individuals may develop personal problems both at home and work. The leader can show sympathetic awareness of this distress together with a desire to alleviate it.

Figure 7.1 *The broad functions of leadership*

in their working groups. A military leader, for example, needs to personify the quality of physical *courage*, one of a cluster of soldierly virtues.

But leadership is more than a general quality of personality and character which can be refracted into a spectrum of 'leadership qualities'. It is also, as I have said, a *role*, determined by the expectations of the group or organization of what they look for in a leader. Studying those expectations allows us to see that there are two strong magnetic poles within them: the leader

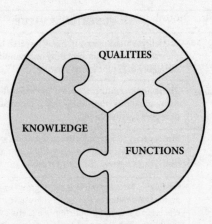

Figure 7.2 *The three elements that blend to make a leader*

is expected to enable the group or organization to fulfil its task or mission *and* to hold it together as an effective working unity. The expectations arrange themselves like iron filings in response to these two poles. That analysis allows us to see that a leader is the kind of person (*qualities*), with the appropriate *knowledge* and *skill* to lead a group to achieve its ends willingly.

This simple concept relates well to the original meaning of our English word *lead*, which comes from *laed*, a word common to all the old North European languages (Dutch, German, Anglo-Saxon, Norwegian, Danish, Swedish) and more or less unchanged within them today. It means a path, road, course of a ship at sea, journey. A leader takes people on a journey, guiding them to their destination. By implication they hold them together as a group, maintaining some sort of order while leading them in the right direction. Mere mountain guides or ships' pilots don't do that. But in Anglo-Saxon (Olde English), we only find the *causative* form of the North European verb *to lead*. In other words, and this is unique to the English language, to lead means to *cause* others – people or animals – to go on a journey.

Note the motivation dimension. Once again, it is not what a mountain guide or ship's pilot is paid to do. How do you *cause* people to make a journey? Be they sheep or soldiers the principle is the same: you lead them forward from in front and they will follow you – freely, willingly, without compulsion. It is simple cause and effect, one known to man for 3,000 years. On an ancient Sumerian clay tablet this proverb was found inscribed: *Soldiers without a king [leader] are like sheep without a shepherd.*

William Shakespeare reveals a clear grasp of this principle. Contrast the armies of the two kings, Macbeth and Henry V. Of Macbeth, troops on the eve of the final decisive battle compare notes and say of his commanders ruefully:

His army moves only by command,
Nothing by love.

The role of leader

The core role of a leader actually refracts into three broad functions derived from the three interactive areas of needs present in all work groups in all domains and levels: the need to achieve the common task, the need to be maintained as a working unity, and the needs which individuals bring into the group by virtue of being individual embodied persons. These three general functions are:

Figure 7.3 *The broad functions of leadership*

This role, of course, has to be fulfilled against a background of a society that has many continuities but is subject to a whole manner of changes that constantly impact on each of the three areas and the organization as a whole.

In order for the three overlapping areas of leadership responsibility to be met, certain more specific functions need to be performed. A *function* is what you *do*, as opposed to a *quality*, which is what you *are*, and also to what you *know*. *Skill* relates to how well you perform the *function*. Here is an indicative or working list of these functions:

Defining the task	What are the purpose, aims and objectives? Why is this work worthwhile?
Planning	A plan answers the question of *how* you are going to get from where you are now to where you want to be. There is nothing like a bad plan to break up a group or frustrate individuals.
Briefing	The ability to communicate, to get across to people the task and the plan.
Controlling	Making sure that all resources and energies are properly harnessed.
Supporting	Setting and maintaining organizational and team values and standards.
Informing	Bringing information to the group and from the group – the *linking* function of leadership.
Reviewing	Establishing and applying the success criteria appropriate to the field.

Levels of leadership

Leadership exists on different levels. Thinking of organizations, there are three broad levels of leadership:

Team   The leader of a team of some 10 to 20 people
              with clearly specified tasks to achieve.

Operational   The leader of one of the main parts of the
              organization and more than one team leader
              are under one's control. It is already a case of
              being a leader of leaders.

Strategic   The leader of a whole organization, with a
              number of operational leaders under one's
              personal direction.

              (*Strategy* derives from two Greek words: *stratos*,
              a large body of people like an army spread out
              in camp, and *egy* – pronounced with an 'h'
              sound and meaning *leader*. The only English
              word we get from it is hegemony.)

A simple recipe for organizational success is to have effective
leaders occupying these roles and working together in
harmony as a team. This is simple enough to say: I'm not
implying that it is easy either to achieve or to maintain this
state of affairs under the pressures of life today, but what is
your alternative?

Within each broad level there may be subdivisions. The
levels also overlap considerably. But the general distinction
above is still worth making as an aid to clear thinking about
organizations – and the needs of leadership development.

Sometimes, however, these three levels of the organizational house are disguised by the elaborate façade of hierarchy. A *hierarchy* (from Greek *hierus* meaning sacred) originally meant a ruling body of priests or clergy organized into orders or ranks, each subordinate to the one above. The Greek *archos* was a generic term for a person who was in authority over others: their leader.

Strategic leadership

The summits of the various kinds of business are, like the tops of mountains, much more alike than the parts below – the bare principles are much the same; it is only the rich variegated details of the lower strata that so contrast with one another. But it needs travelling to know that the summits are the same. Those who live on one mountain believe that their mountain is wholly unlike all others.

WALTER BAGEHOT, BRITISH JOURNALIST, ESSAYIST
AND BUSINESSMAN

The leadership role, as I have mentioned above, has evolved in response to the three interlocking areas of need present in all working groups or organizations. At strategic level the broad functions of achieving the task, building the team and developing the individual which constitute it can be broken down further into seven generic functions, rather like light refracted into seven colours of the rainbow:

- Giving direction for the organization as a whole;

- Strategic thinking and strategic planning;

- Making it happen;

- Relating the parts to the whole;

- Building the key partnerships and other social relationships;

- Releasing the corporate spirit;

- Choosing and developing leaders for today and tomorrow.

Strategic leadership differs not in kind but in magnitude of issues and scale of complexity encountered. It calls for a commensurate level of what the Greeks called *phronesis*, practical wisdom.

The hourglass model

The hourglass model of career change which I introduced some time ago throws more light on levels of leadership. Some people in organizations, I suggest, follow career paths that resemble an inverted funnel. They begin broad-based at school, then choose between Arts and Sciences, before specializing still further. The process is repeated or continued at university and in postgraduate training, especially in the science-based and vocationally orientated courses. Again, the process is repeated or refined further when a person enters employment: he or she is – or will soon become – a specialist. Some people will remain – and develop – as specialists for the rest of their careers.

For many other specialists, however, becoming a manager fits in with their career plans. Their potential for 'getting results through people' may have been evident to them for a long time or it might have been first identified in the selection process of the organization in question. Whichever way, they *want* to be managers or leaders.

At that point in their careers they are moving through the narrow neck of the hourglass – it may have been long or short in

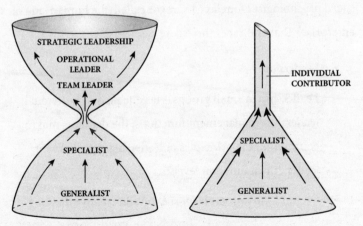

Figure 7.4 *The hourglass model of career change*

their cases – and they are becoming generalists again. The degree to which they will retain a specialist contribution to the output of the organization clearly varies from domain to domain, but their role has been altered: the new generalist role as *leader* should now be their priority.

Two 'widening' processes need to occur if a person emerging from the narrow neck is to advance eventually to a strategic leadership role. First, their knowledge of the enterprise as a whole – finance and marketing, production and distribution in the case of industry – needs to be developed and consolidated, partly by business courses but also by the broadening experience of working in more than one area of the organization's operations.

The second development – often neglected – is a growth of the understanding and competence in what the American social psychologist Douglas McGregor called 'the human side of enterprise'. That embraces three core elements:

- *Leadership*

  Leadership in small groups – task, team and individual; leadership/management functions; the decision-making continuum; the principles of leadership development; leadership at different levels;

- *Decision-making, problem-solving and creative thinking*

The classic process of making decisions; the element of effective thinking; problem-solving techniques; creative or innovative thinking – how to do it and how to encourage it in others;

- *Communication*

  The two-way nature of communication; non-verbal communication; the four skills of speaking, listening, writing and reading; meetings; downwards, upwards and lateral communication in large organizations.

To this list should be added a fourth candidate: time management. The principles of time management should apply to everyone, specialist and manager alike, but a reminder of those principles, together with such tips and rules of thumb which exist, is timely and fitting when a person becomes a manager. If you can't manage your own time in order to be effective as possible then you can't manage anything or anyone else either.

Strategic thinking and judgment

Strategic thinking is concerned with the medium- and long-term future, with all of its possibilities, uncertainties and complexities.

Therefore, it requires calm reflection and judgment for, as a strategic leader, your prime responsibility is to ensure that your organization is going in the right direction. That sounds simple enough but it's not always easy to achieve. What *is* the right strategic direction? How or where do you establish it? Why is implementation so difficult?

We can break the problem into two parts: identifying the best strategy and pursuing it to the desired result. Although these two parts in reality are interwoven, it makes sense to separate out the *thinking* side of it from the *implementation* phases of action.

It is also useful, I think, to distinguish between such *strategic thinking* on the one hand and *strategic planning* on the other. Strategic thinking is thinking about the longer term and the more important ends in any situation – including your own life – and the pathways that may or may not lead to them. If and when you can identify such an end or set of ends, and choose among the possible pathways the ones that make most sense, the process of corporate planning can get under way. It is unwise to launch into a strategic planning exercise before your strategic thought has come to some clear working conclusions, although, believe me, this does happen.

To remind you, *strategy* in Ancient Greek meant the *whole* art of a commander-in-chief, including leadership, administration and working with allies, as well as knowing how to bring an enemy to battle and what tactics to employ. Strategy, if you like, was the thinking of a *strategos*, a general.

Importance	To be able to distinguish between the important, the less important and the unimportant is the starting point. If it is important, it is marked by, or possesses, weight or consequence. It has evident value, either generally or in particular relation, and often by merely existing.
Longer term	How long is long? That all depends. But *strategic* implies a longer-term perspective rather than the short-term view. Indeed, to think strategically may mean trading short-term gain for long-term advantage.

In the military context, General Alanbrooke, who served as the head of the British Army, Churchill's chief-of-staff and his principal military adviser for most of the Second World War, declared that the objects of strategy are:

...to determine the aim, which should be political: to derive from that aim a series of military objectives to be achieved: to assess these objectives as to the military requirements they create, and the pre-conditions which the achievement of each is likely to necessitate: to measure available and potential resources against the requirements and to chart from this process a coherent pattern of priorities and a rational course of action.

In an earlier book also entitled *The Art of Judgment* (1969), Sir Geoffrey Vickers made the seminal point that all the ends we pursue can be expressed in terms of changes in relation. To defeat an enemy, for example, if you happened to be a Roman general, meant that the vanquished entered into a new relation with you – slavery. The wealth and land you plundered and conquered gave you wealth, which changed your relation with others in a thousand direct or subtle ways. Or at least you might hope it would do so. Fame also changed your relative position in the list of those competing for high office in Rome. When in doubt, it is sometimes useful to ask yourself, what's the end-state change in relation with something or somebody that I'm seeking in this situation?

This clarity of freshness of vision – seeing the situation steadily as a whole with all its complex elements but also discerning its essentials – calls for what the Japanese call the *sunao* mind. Konosuke Matsushita, one of the most celebrated Japanese business leaders of the last century, strove for it all his life, as his close associate Toru Yamaguchi writes:

The *sunao* mind or the untrapped mind is calm and highly adaptable. It enables its owner to free himself of preconceived notions so that he can see things as they are. Managers who don't have the *sunao* mind are often swayed by their own interests in decision-making, inevitably leading to corporate failure. Since managers, just like everyone else, are creatures of habit and prejudice, they have to cultivate the *sunao* mind to judge the situation accurately and lead the way to corporate success. Konosuke always said that cultivating the *sunao* mind is important, and that it wasn't easy, but he continued to his final days the constant work of developing it.

A common judgment call: Timing the pace of change

Changing things is central to leadership. Changing them before anyone else is creative leadership.
ORDWAY TEAD, US AUTHOR AND EDUCATOR

Organizational culture is strategically important, partly as the end in itself and partly as the means to an end – your overall success strategy. What is certain is that it will need to be changed, for a culture that is static is already moribund.

Change, however, is a very broad concept. It embraces any variation, whether affecting a thing superficially or essentially. It covers in the same word a loss of original identity of a substitution of one thing for another and quite trivial alterations. Indeed, *any* process of variation, slight or great, in appearance or essence, in quality or quantity, is signified by change.

After your first hundred days as a strategic leader you should have a good idea of what differences you want to make – the changes that are, in your view, necessary or desirable. If you are involved in a business organization, these may include changes in products and marketing strategy, in the organizational structure that balances the parts and the whole, and in the composition of the top team. But, with the fresh eye of a newcomer, you may sense the need for a deeper change, a change in 'the way we do things', and consequently in the way the organization thinks. You are now on the borders of the organizational culture, which may well be guarded by a number of 'Keep Out' signs.

Changing the organizational culture is a very slow business in an organization with a culture adverse to change. 'Do I really *have* to change?' is the silent cry. Of course, if an organization *has* to change, it will – at the last minute, truculently and with many a complaint. When panic really sets in, the response to change suddenly switches from '*Over my dead body*' to '*Let's do it overnight.*'

Abraham Lincoln used to tell a story about a frog that fell into a deep, muddy wagon track. A couple of days later, he was still there. Frog friends found him and urged him to get out of his predicament. He made a few feeble efforts, but remained mired in his rut.

For the next few days, his friends kept encouraging him to try harder, but they finally gave up and went back to their pond.

The next day the frog was seen sunning himself contentedly beside the edge of the pond.

'How did you get out of the rut?' his friends asked.

'Well, as you know,' said the frog, 'I couldn't but a wagon came along and I *had* to.'

The problem with Lincoln's frog is that inordinate delay in changing left him only one option. As a general principle, the sooner an organization is willing to change – ahead, that is, of the time it *has* to change – the more options it has open to it. Instead of being forced, change becomes proactive in nature and aimed at securing the heights of advantage.

In changing *ahead of time* you gain some solid advantages. Most organizations in any field have a herd instinct: they stick close together and only change when they are following suit or catching up. Organizations that are leaders in their field (is that not in *your* vision?) are pioneers – they change first before any others. So, take change by the hand and lead it where you want it to go before it takes you by the throat and drags you in any direction.

Planned change **Change forced by external factors**

MANY   FEW
OPTIONS   OPTIONS   NO OPTIONS

Proactive	Sense of Urgency	Reactive
• Good communication	• Have to focus – can't do all the good things you would like	• 'Catch-up'
• Involvement	• Trying to keep up with competition	• Trying to do too many things at once
• Training for new ways	• Doing the same things everybody else is doing	• Falling behind the competition
• Anticipating the customer needs		• Driven by short-term, crisis decisions which change frequently
• Staying ahead of competition		

Figure 7.5 *Planned change versus change forced by external factors*

The necessity to change ahead of a Lincoln's frog jump, and the change that is both necessary or desirable in terms of vision and values, should form a major theme as a communicator within your organization.

The product of good leadership

How can you improve your powers as a team-builder, given the complexities, potential problems and challenges outlined above? The answer is simple: form a clear concept in your mind of what an excellent team looks like. Then, like an automatic pilot, that concept will serve to guide you in all that you do and say to achieve it.

High-performance teams at every level – and the organization as a whole working as one big team – have certain clearly recognizable hallmarks. Hallmarks (from Goldsmiths' Hall in London, where gold and silver articles were assayed and stamped) are literally the official marks stamped on gold and silver articles in England to attest their purity. What, then, are the hallmarks distinguishing the 'still more excellent' teams? Here is an indicative list of them. I say 'indicative', because you are welcome to add or subtract from it.

- *Clear, realistic and challenging objectives*

  The team is focused on what has to be done – broken down into stretching but feasible goals, both team and individual. Everyone knows what is expected of him or her;

- *Shared sense of purpose*

  This doesn't mean that the team can recite the mission statement in unison! Here, the purpose is energy plus direction – what engineers call a vector. It should animate and invigorate the whole team. All share a sense of ownership and responsibility for team success;

- *Best use of resources*

  A high-performance team means that resources are allocated for strategic reasons for the good of the whole. They are not seen as the private property of any part of the organization. Resources include people and their time, not just money and material;

- *Progress review*

  The willingness to monitor their own progress and to generate improvements characterizes excellent teams. These improvements encompass process – *how* we work together – as well as tasks – *what* we do together;

- *Building on experience*

  A blame culture mars any team. Errors will be made, but
  the greatest error of all is to do nothing so as to avoid
  making any! A wise team learns from failure, realizing
  that success teaches us nothing and continual success
  may breed arrogance;

- *Mutual trust and support*

  A good team trusts its members to pursue their part
  in the common task. Appreciation is expressed and
  recognition given. People play to each other's strengths
  and cover each other's weaknesses;

- *Communication*

  People listen to one another and build on one
  another's contributions. They communicate openly,
  freely and with skill (clear, concise, simple and
  with tact). Issues, problems and weaknesses are not
  sidestepped. Differences of opinion are respected.
  Team members know when to be very supportive
  and sensitive, and when to challenge and be
  intellectually tough;

- *Riding out the storms*

  In times of turbulent change, it is never going to
  be all plain sailing. When the inevitable storms

and crises arise, an excellent team rises to the
challenge and demonstrates its sterling worth.
It has resilience.

Where these eight hallmarks – in no order of importance – are
present, people enjoy working together as a team more deeply.
They have fun, like other teams, but so rare is the experience
of working in an excellent team that the enjoyment and fun
are transformed with hindsight into the true gold and silver of
enduring satisfaction and a sense of gratitude.

Leadership, in summary, is simple but never easy. It calls for
your wholehearted commitment. The most deeply compelled
action is also the freest one. By that, I mean, no part of you is
outside the action.

A LEADER IS A BRIDGE

IN THE MEDIEVAL WELSH LEGEND called The Mabinogion, a
collection of ancient tales, is the story of a prince leading an army to
free his sister. The forces fleeing from him cross a river and then break
all the bridges. The prince, a giant of a man, laid himself across the river
and his soldiers used him as their bridge. This story gives us the great
Welsh proverb

A fo ben bid bont –

'HE WHO WOULD LEAD, LET HIM BE A BRIDGE'

It was the motto of the Pantglas Junior School in Aberfan, South
Wales, scene of the disaster in 1966 when a slag heap collapsed

and engulfed a school, killing 116 children and 28 adults. The motto provided the inspiration for the logo adopted by the community of a bridge and flaming torch, symbolic of its reconciling work and the passing on of the experiences and lessons to others. The words are wise, inspiring and humbling for any who aspire to leadership.

Key points: Leadership – your second vocation

- Vocation is the matrix of true leadership. For vocational people tend to fulfil the first necessary condition for a leader, namely that they possess the characteristics admired or respected in their field or domain. They don't have a problem with credibility, nor do they lack enthusiasm;

- Vocational people are often creative pioneers in their field, going into territory where no one has gone before. If they attract followers on the path that they blazon, then they find themselves – often to their surprise – being looked upon as leaders;

- In corporate or organizational life, the other side of the leadership coin – the ability to make everyone partners in the common enterprise – becomes equally important.

Providing direction, leading by example, teambuilding and team-working, motivating and inspiring others, are integral to the role of leadership;

- The 'untrapped mind' is open enough to see many possibilities, humble enough to learn from anyone and everything, perceptive enough to see things as they really are, and wise enough to judge their true value;

- *Strategia* or strategy is the generic art of any leader-in-chief. As the Chinese proverb goes, *There are many paths to the top of the mountain, but the view is always the same*. A strategic leader, you will have noted, is always 'a leader of leaders', a phrase borrowed from Ovid's *Heroides*;

- Strategy in the narrower sense is the thinking appropriate to the strategic leader and applies to all aspects of their responsibility. As it calls for above-average judgment – as such – it cannot be taught like a science or skill, but like any art, it can be learned by those who aspire to master it;

- Imperturbability is a quality expected of true leaders at all levels. It means coolness and presence of mind under all circumstances. *Calm* and *collected* are often paired in a phrase to suggest the complete intactness of mental resources in the face of difficulty. *Calm* stresses a quiet approach to a problem, devoid of hysterical actions or utterances, while *collected* stresses the application of appropriate mental or physical effort to the solution of the problem: to remain *calm* and *collected* in the midst of a noisy demonstration.

The task of leadership is not to put greatness into people, but to elicit it, for the greatness is there already.

JOHN BUCHAN

8

How to share decisions

*If you worked with Einstein he made you aware of a common
enemy – the problem. And you became his partner in battle.*
BANESH HOFFMANN, BRITISH MATHEMATICIAN AND PHYSICIST

INTO THE MINDS of leaders in any sphere of life there
must enter a constant question: 'How far should I share my
decisions with other members of the group or organization?'
Any approach to decision-making today would be incomplete
if it treated the process purely as an intellectual exercise by
the leader, one that did not involve other people. Certainly,
the pressures that are on managers to share decisions are
considerable. There is a general if uneven desire throughout the
world for greater participation, and that means participation in
the decisions which affect the working lives of those concerned.
How far should people share in decisions within all human
enterprises and purposeful contexts?

Your first step to greater effectiveness with reference to sharing decisions is to become fully aware of the range of generic options open to you. Here they are:

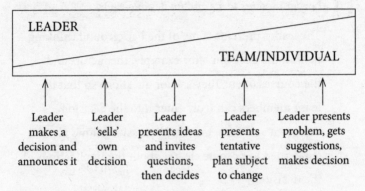

Figure 8.1 *The decision-making spectrum of options*

Some brief notes on these options:

1 *Leader makes decision and announces it*

Having reviewed the 'courses of action' in light of the aim or objective and the prevailing factors, the leader selects one course and tells his or her team members their decision. How they will react may have come into their calculations, but they have no direct share in the decision-process.

2 *Leader makes decision and 'sells' it*

Here, the leader makes the decision, announces it and goes to give the reasons for it, and to state the advantages that accrue from it to the team members. Implicitly, they are recognizing their importance in implementing the decision.

3 *Leader presents ideas and invites questions*

The leader presents some of the background thinking behind the decision – for example, the factors and the courses open. They ask for questions so that the team members can truly enter into the decision, explore it and accept it. The discussion allows all concerned to become clearer about the implications of the decision.

4 *Leader presents a tentative decision subject to change*

The proposed decision is offered for discussion and review. Having heard the comments and questions from those who will be affected by it, the leader makes the final decision.

5 *Leader presents problem, gets suggestions, then decides*

The leader identifies the problem or the option of courses of action which lead towards the goal, and comes before the team members without his mind being weighted towards any one solution or plan.

The function of the group becomes one of increasing the leader's repertory of possible solutions to the problem. The purpose is to capitalize on the knowledge and experience of those present. From the expanded list of options developed by the leader and his team members in discussion, the leader then selects the course of action that he or she regards as the optimum one in the circumstances.

SHARING DECISIONS		
Degree of participation	Useful	Not useful
1 You present a tentative plan subject to change if another in the group comes up with a better one.	When group time is short. Where you have much experience in the field and are fairly sure you are right.	Where time is plentiful and the group is as technically competent as you are. When you are only going through the motions, being unwilling to accept any changes.
2 You present the problem and get suggestions from the group.	It involves the group much more than (1). Groups can be far more creative than their individual members – including you. ('Two heads are better than one').	Can be time-consuming, if the group lacks sufficient knowledge and interest in the matter in hand.
3 You present a firm plan, subject to only minor changes of detail to improve it.	When you are absolutely sure that you are right. Where time is critically short.	Where the group needs to be more involved in the thinking and deciding if it is to be really committed to action.

In making the judgment of how or where to decide on this continuum, there are two key factors to be taken into account: *time* and *people*.

In some situations, time is of the essence. Indeed, in organizations or groups which work characteristically in crisis situations (ones in which by definition time is in very short supply and where – often – there is a life-or-death dimension) leaders tend to make decisions and announce them. Moreover, as research at the scenes of road accidents and forest fires reveals, people expect decisive and firm direction from one person – they need it.

The second key factor is the people or person involved. What knowledge and experience do they possess? Are they qualified or competent in any way to contribute to the decision? Clearly, there is a great deal of difference between making a decision where none of those present have any knowledge or background relevant to the matter in hand, and making one where all concerned are conversant, experienced and competent. For this reason the higher the level of decisions in organizations, the more they tend towards the right-hand end of the decision-making spectrum. For there is always that fundamental principle at work here: *the more that people share in decisions which affect their working lives, the more they are committed to carrying them out*. It is also applicable to families.

The nature of consensus

Harold Wilson, twice Prime Minister of the UK, in a letter to me written in his retirement, emphasized the importance of gaining consensus at the highest level in any essentially democratic society. 'Leadership,' he wrote, 'itself must vary in different areas of life. In politics you are leading a group of MPs who have been elected in their own right by their constituencies. You have to carry them with you by argument and consent… But in politics as in most other walks of life, the leader who gets too far ahead, or too way out, may find themselves on their own.'

Helmut Schmidt, a very effective Chancellor of West Germany, once commented on the unique challenge of being a democratic leader: 'It is an enormous piece of art to be a leader, but not to appear a leader. It needs feelings in the tips of the fingers.'

A leader is best,
When people are hardly aware of his existence,
Not so good when people praise his government,
Less good when people stand in fear,
Worst, when people are contemptuous.
Fail to honour people, and they will fail to honour you.
But a good leader, who speaks little,
When his task is accomplished, his work done,
The people say, 'We did it ourselves!'

LAO TZU, SEVENTH-CENTURY BCE

Granted a common commitment among group members to the purpose and aims of the organization – a shared set of values – and an absence of aggressive or arrogant egoism in individual group members, consensus is usually forthcoming if a leader seeks it with patience, determination and skill. Here is a working definition of *consensus* (from the Latin word for agreement):

> When the feasible courses of action have been debated thoroughly by the group and everyone is prepared to accept that in the circumstances one particular solution is the best way forward, even though it might not be *every* person's preferred solution. The most important test is that everyone is prepared to *act* as though it was their preferred course of action.

There is a skill in testing for the presence of real consensus, either with another individual or within a group. Where those in positions of leadership lack that skill, there is always a danger that consensus will be falsely assumed – often with dire consequences.

As the Chinese saying goes, *A thousand workers, a thousand plans*. To get anything agreed and done calls for leadership. When all people feel themselves to be equal in value or worth, if not in knowledge or experience, that is when true leadership is needed. Where you cannot issue orders like a drill sergeant, the skills of identifying and creating consensus become even more important. As Montesquieu wrote, 'To suggest where you cannot compel, to guide where you cannot demand, that is the supreme form of skill.' Here, humility and skill go hand-in-hand.

FROM STRONG ARGUMENT TO WHOLE-HEARTED ACCEPTANCE OF THE CONSENSUS

EISENHOWER RECALLS HOW CHURCHILL WAS a powerful persuader in his endeavour to convince others that he was right, but once the best decision was made – whether or not it followed his line – he always gave it his complete support:

> Indeed Churchill's skill in the use of words and logic was so great that on several occasions when he and I disagreed on some important matter – even when I was convinced of the correctness of my own view and when responsibility was clearly mine – I had a very hard time withstanding his arguments.
>
> More than once he forced me to re-examine my own premises, to convince myself again that I was right – or accept his solution. Yet if the decision went against him, he accepted it with good grace, and did everything in his power to support it with proper action. Leadership by persuasion and the wholehearted acceptance of a contrary decision are both fundamentals of democracy.

The importance of listening to specialists

Just before the Battle of Badr in 624 CE, Muhammad accompanied by an advance guard set out to secure the nearest well to Badr from the direction of Medina. Once there, they halted to rest, but a poor Bedouin warrior named Hubab al-Jamuh of the Bani Salama, who was in the party and knew the area well, approached the Prophet.

'Is this a place which God has ordered you to occupy,' he asked, 'so that we can neither advance nor withdraw from it, or is it a matter of opinion and military tactics?'

Muhammad replied that it was the latter. Then Hubab pointed out to him that it was not the right place to stop: they should press on to the well nearest to the enemy, halt there and stop up the wells behind it. For themselves, they should construct a cistern so that they would have plenty of water. Then they could fight their enemy, who would have nothing to drink. The Prophet said that this was an excellent plan and agreed to it. They acted upon it immediately: the wells were stopped, a cistern built and filled with water from which his men replenished their drinking vessels.

The immediate preliminaries of Badr, when about 300 Muslims faced over 1,000 well-armed Meccans in battle and defeated them, gives us another vivid glimpse of Muhammad in action as a leader. Note his calmness and confidence, doubtless based upon a complete trust in Allah. Leaders who smile and joke in the face of such odds release the tension in their soldiers; they radiate confidence.

In this story Muhammad is in the role of a leader of a faith-community of Islam. Although there is some evidence that as a boy, he had been present at one desert battle between rival Bedouin tribes, at that stage he had no military experience of warfare, let alone military command. Hubab, by contrast, was doubtless a veteran of many desert raids and battles. Muhammad listened to him as one who knew what he was talking about and acted promptly upon his advice. This just shows how good judgment of people can compensate for lack of professional or technical knowledge or experience.

By definition almost, as a strategic leader you are a generalist. You may not understand all the complexities of advanced finance or the mysteries of high technology. To do the 'establishing the truth' part of the judgment process, you will have to consult others. Yet, like the Prophet Muhammad with Hubab al-Jamuh, you have to be able to gauge the degree of authority – the authority of knowledge – in the advice or opinions of those who are worth listening to.

Remember, you will always have at least a little knowledge about the matter in question, otherwise you would not be where you are. Use it to assess your adviser's more specialized knowledge. If there is an apparent conflict between what you are being told and what you sense to be the case, sort it out. Don't be afraid to ask questions that will give you a reasonably accurate idea of the length, depth, height and width of this person's knowledge. Don't make false assumptions about the other person's expertise. Have they been reliable in the past? Do they have a reputation for honesty and integrity? Can you trust them to tell you the truth, however unpalatable it may be?

Bad advisers will feed your interpretations of the situation that are far from objective or value-free. They want you to follow a particular course, and they feed you information to support their interpretation of reality. Conflicting evidence is put into the footnote; other options relegated to the appendices.

President John F. Kennedy's decision in 1961 to countenance and support an invasion of Cuba by Cuban dissidents based in Florida – the Bay of Pigs affair – provides a classic example of how advisers with their own interests and objectives in mind can exercise a harmful influence on decision-making. The organization urging him to attempt the abortive invasion of Cuba by proxy – the Central Intelligence Agency – also happened to be the department supplying him with information about Cuba and the Cubans. You can guess what happened. This fact does not excuse President Kennedy, of course. He had some knowledge from other sources, such as the newspapers. He should have made a judgment about the experts and the degree to which they could be expected to be impartial or disinterested. At least he learnt his lessons and dealt with the subsequent Cuban missile crisis in a far more effective way.

In consequence, a priority for anyone in a strategic leadership position should be to place a premium on being a *truth-led organization*. Discourage anyone who seeks to supply you with filtered or distorted information in order to support their preferred course of action. Create an atmosphere where everyone is committed to finding the truth and acting upon it. Be willing to admit that you are wrong if the truth compels you to do so. In doing so, you will not only show courage, but also set a good example to others around and below you.

Here is an illuminating example. It is about a comparatively little-known scientist called R.V. Jones in the Second World War, who was called upon to give specialist advice to Prime Minister Winston Churchill. See if you can think of managers who match up to this story in the quality of truth-seeking in decision-making they exhibit, whether they are in the position of the chief executive (Churchill) or of the specialist adviser (Jones).

CHURCHILL AS CREATIVE THINKER

SIR WINSTON CHURCHILL ALWAYS HAD a soft spot for what in those days were often called the 'backroom boys'. As Chancellor of the Exchequer in the 1920s he would summon Sir Ralph Hawtrey, the Treasury's financial and economic expert, with the instruction, according to his private secretary P.J. Grigg, that 'The learned man should be released from the dungeon in which we were said to have immured him, have his chains struck off and the straw brushed from his hair and clothes, and be admitted to the light and warmth of an argument in the Treasury boardroom with the greatest living master of argument.'

During his period as Prime Minister during the Second World War, Sir Winston's favourite 'boffin' – a scientist employed by the government – was a young, softly spoken scientist called Dr R.V. Jones. The Prime Minister would summon him from the headquarters of MI6 across St James's Park.

Reg Jones made his great breakthrough on 21 June 1940. With his team he had been puzzling over radio beams transmitted from Germany during bomber raids over England and became convinced they were a navigation device for steering aircraft to their targets. Some senior scientists were highly sceptical, refusing to believe that beams could be bent around the earth's surface. Jones believed they could, and what's more, that they could be bent again by countermeasures in order to redirect the aerial raiders away from urban areas to drop their bombs over open country.

That morning, Jones entered his office to find a message instructing him to come to the Cabinet Room at No. 10 Downing Street. Suspecting revenge for a practical joke, he thought little of it but checked and found the message was genuine. He arrived 25 minutes late.

At one point in the meeting Churchill asked him to elaborate a point of detail. Instead, he spoke for 20 minutes. 'The few minutes of desultory discussion that had ensued after my entry showed me that nobody else knew as much about the matter as I did myself,' he recalled later, 'and, although I was not conscious of my calmness at the time, the very gravity of the situation seemed to generate the steady nerve for which it called.'

Reg Jones made a lasting impression on the Prime Minister. Thereafter, Churchill swore by him as 'the man who broke the bloody beam' – heady stuff for a 28-year-old.

'The first thing was to be absolutely scrupulous in trying to establish the truth,' Jones said as he recalled his meetings with Churchill. 'Winston said: "You don't have to be polite, you just have to be right." If you got somebody, however eminent, and asked him three successive "Why's?", there were not many people who could stand up to it. It was quite astonishing how shaky their knowledge base was. It was the old story of 99 per cent perspiration and one per cent inspiration. One needed a very sound grounding in basic principles and a mistrust of elaborate argument when something simple would do.'

To summarize, as a listening leader you should be open to unsolicited advice if it comes from someone who possesses the authority of knowledge in a particular domain – but don't lose your critical faculty.

There is a pleasing story of a cobbler who detected a fault in a shoe lacing in a painting by Apelles, a famous Greek painter in the days of Alexander the Great. The artist rectified the fault. The cobbler then ventured to criticize the way that Apelles had painted the legs of the people in the picture, but Apelles responded swiftly: 'Keep to your trade. You understand about shoes, but not about anatomy.'

Key points: How to share decisions

- The Japanese word *nemawashi* for a group meeting means literally 'to loosen the roots of a tree'. Group discussion before an important decision – if properly guided – should lead to a clear understanding of the situation, the issues at stake and the feasible options for action;

- The chief reason for sharing decisions with your team as far as it is possible to do so is simple: The more that people share in decisions that affect their lives, the more they will be motivated or committed to implement them wholeheartedly;

- Always listen to specialists, provided they really do know what they are talking about. In that context it helps greatly if you are a good judge of people;

- Listen with an open mind, but never allow others to do your thinking for you. As a leader, you are being paid to exercise your judgment;

- You need a clear idea when it comes to what consensus is and what it isn't. Finding out whether or not consensus is present in a meeting is partly a matter of observation and partly intuition. If in doubt, test for it;

- 'A genuine leader is not a searcher for consensus, but a moulder of consensus,' said Martin Luther King in his address at the Episcopal National Cathedral in Washington (31 March 1968);

- As a leader, it is your job to see that the right decision is made – you can't delegate that responsibility to the group, so remain in charge of the process and remember that it is you – not the group – who is accountable for the outcome.

Transcendent common sense is the rare power of seeing things as they are, which signifies genius. It is the ability to draw right conclusions and take correct action.

J.W. FORTESCUE, WRITING ABOUT THE DUKE OF WELLINGTON

9

The role of values

We navigated by the same stars.

WINSTON CHURCHILL,
SPEAKING OF PRESIDENT DE GAULLE

ULTIMATELY, IT IS our values that give us the stars by which we navigate ourselves through life. It is self-evident that they play a key role in any process of judgment, personal or corporate. Therefore, to adapt a famous saying said to be engraved above the entrance of the temple at Delphi: *Know your values*.

Values (in the plural) are your principles or standards; your judgment of what is valuable or important in life. A *value* indicates characteristically something (as a principle or quality) intrinsically valuable or desirable. If a person is described as seeking only material values rather than human values, we all know roughly what that means.

Our values seem to inhabit our subconscious or even unconscious minds. Sometimes it is as if they are only aroused or awakened to life after some particular situation. Conscience pangs can operate like that, suggesting that in Shakespeare's words (*Henry V*, Act VI, Scene I):

> *There is some soul of goodness in things evil,*
> *Would men observingly distil it out.*

Albert von Speer, the top industrial manager in Hitler's Germany, is a classic example of a buried conscience coming to life. His book, *Inside the Third Reich* (1970), contains a confession of his suppressed awareness of good and evil in relation to Hitler's Nazi policy for exterminating the Jews. Historians have debated how far Speer's remorse was genuine, but my brother, Colonel Paul Adair, who conducted a video interview with Speer on behalf of the Ministry of Defence, was convinced – and convinced me – that he was indeed sincere.

> It is true that as a favourite and later as one of Hitler's most influential ministers I was isolated. It is also true that the habit of thinking within the limits of my own field provided me, both as architect and as Armaments Minister, with many opportunities for evasion. It is true that I did not know what was really beginning on November 9, 1938, and what ended in Auschwitz and Maidanek. But on the final analysis I myself

determined the degree of my isolation, the extremity of my evasions, and the extent of my ignorance.

I therefore know today that my agonised self-examinations posed the question as wrongly as did the questioners whom I have met since my release. Whether I knew or did not know, or how much or how little I knew, is totally unimportant when I consider what horrors I ought to have known about and what conclusions would have been the natural ones to draw from the little I did know. Those who ask me are fundamentally expecting me to offer justifications. But I have none. No apologies are possible…

An American historian has said of me that I loved machines more than people. He is not wrong. I realise that the sight of suffering people influenced only my emotions, but not my conduct. On the plane of feelings only sentimentality emerged; in the realm of decisions, on the other hand, I continued to be ruled by the principles of utility. In the Nuremberg Trial the indictment against me was based on the use of prisoners in the armaments factories.

Gone for ever with these words is the belief that technologists or scientists could ever abdicate their moral responsibilities, or disclaim a concern with personal values. Rather, conscience should be accepted for what it is, the radar system of a fundamentally good person. Like other signals, its messages can be ignored, jammed or wilfully misinterpreted. But to allow conscience to atrophy through such abuse can lead to trouble, and ultimately, its retrospective self-condemnations.

Far better to see it as a moral awareness, designed to allow us to avoid the grievous agony of guilt. For conscience is a friendly poltergeist. As novelist George MacDonald noted about one of his fictional characters: 'She was sorely troubled with what is, by huge discourtesy, called a bad conscience – being in reality a conscience doing its duty so well that it makes the whole house uncomfortable.'

Some values are relative, some are absolute. Don't fall into the trap of trying to define the indefinable. Abstract nouns such as we find in any discussions of values stand for properties that cannot be defined in any other terms. For example, the world has no accepted definition of love, but we know what it is and it is the star that guides us in all our personal relations.

Social capitalism

In an earlier book of mine, *Management and Morality: The Problems and Opportunities of Social Capitalism* (1974), I identified a pattern or framework of values which together acted as stars in the corporate firmament. Over 40 years later, they are still there before us, shining brightly. *Social Capitalism*, the phrase first coined in that book, stood then – as it stands now – for the confluence of four sets of values: *economic*, *social*, *individual* and *environmental*.

- *Money*

  Valued both as a means of exchange and as a store of wealth (purchasing power). Profit in business is necessary; no one wants to work in a business that is making a loss;

  Money or wealth is not an evil, it all depends upon how it is gained and to what use it is put;

- *Society*

  Valued as the human community: local, regional, national and global;

  We all live in a wider 'community of interests and diversity of talents'. That wide community – society at large – is the ocean in which all organizations move, live and have their being;

- *Individual*

  Valued by virtue of the fact that we are all *individual embodied persons*. All persons are ends as well as means. All persons, by virtue of their personhood, have significance or value;

Organizations, for example, that tolerate bullying or sexual harassment are committing sins against the personhood – or to use a rarer but apt word – the *personeity* of their employees;

- *Nature*

Valued as our natural environment, the source of all our material resources but also as an end in itself, and one not without beauty. As the phenomenon of climate change is revealing, the natural environment is fragile; it is vulnerable to the devastating effects of old-style Capitalism.

In our long history, each of these values – *money, society,* the *individual* and *nature* – have claimed or been accorded a quasi-religious status as the supreme end of life and therefore to be the dominant motive for work. Disinfected from the aura of divinity, each has 'floated' as a value against the other three values, recognized but yet to be more deeply felt in our increasingly global or world-wide community. And their old 'theologies' have become secular subjects: Economics, Sociology, Psychology and Ecology.

In the *Director*, the journal of the Institute of Directors in the UK, Sir Adrian Cadbury wrote this thoughtful review of *Management and Morality*:

THE STANDARD OF BUSINESS CONDUCT

JOHN ADAIR QUOTES LORD ASHBY as saying 'Industry will make a great mistake if it neglects the stirring of a change in values in society.' He takes us through the implications of those changes for managers and spends time on the precise definition of the words we use in discussing issues like social responsibility. I found the clarity of his analysis helpful and I have a better chart to judge my position by as a result of reading *Management and Morality*.

The book is in two parts: the first half establishes the framework within which managers have to take moral decisions and the second half looks at guidelines for action. As John Adair points out, the difficult decisions are not between right and wrong, but between different combinations of right. To judge these, we need to be aware of our own set of values and to be able to compare them with those of our fellow managers. He is therefore in favour of relevant case studies rather than general philosophical guides.

In addition to helping the individual manager, the book is concerned with raising the general standard of business conduct. Adair offers four ways forward: the revision of company law, a code of corporate conduct (probably as an annexe to the law), more non-executive directors on boards and the more effective participation of shareholders.

I would expect to see progress in all four fields, but I believe that the best guardians of standards of business morality are our own good opinions of ourselves and our wish to stand well with our peers. As John Bentley says in the book, 'I'm fed up not being liked.' All of which underlines the importance of information disclosure and open reporting in raising standards.

Adair concludes: 'The moral leadership of industry and commerce remains firmly in the seats around the boardroom table.' That being so, we had better understand what those words mean.

Now nearly half a century has elapsed since Cadbury wrote these words. Since then, how would you assess the progress of global social capitalism? What still needs to be done?

Disagreements abound on the relative placings of the values, both in general and in particular situations. There is a growing consensus, however, that all of them *ought* to be taken into account in political and managerial decision-making. And the grounds for this *ought* conviction are both moral and practical, in a now inseparable mixture.

Attempts to produce an integrating purpose for industry to span the still-existing gap are symptoms of this development. To 'create wealth', for example, is more in accord with social capitalism than to 'accumulate profits'. The former can imply a social reference, the other is a relic of the old-style capitalism.

Social capitalism is certainly more than a matter of words: it represents an important and continuing shift in the value system of our common life. Strictly speaking, there are no new values, for values are timeless. But our valuing faculties are now more sensitive to a whole range of values impinging upon business and industrial working life.

One characteristic early form of expressing the emerging value system of social capitalism, still fairly common, simply listed the human interests now to be taken into account in decision-making: shareholders, customers, employees, consumers and even competitors.

A second generation of form is distinguished by a stress upon the company as a community, microcosm of society, with a necessity to confirm to its minimum legal standards for good conduct and with a certain freedom to be actually better than the social average. In an early expression of it, in 1961, the second Henry Ford could declare:

> A corporation may be primarily a producer of goods, but it is more than just that; it is a small society within society, one with motivations, with rules and principles of its own. It is a purposeful organization that can and must give more than just money to those who serve it, and those it serves. It should reflect in its daily actions the principles and aspirations of our society in its finest tradition.

Social capitalism is as incomplete as a child. To some extent it is unfolding predictably, as if according to a genetic code of values which are the stored essences of human history in our present consciousness, yet there remains a large area of freedom. There are choices to be made; each decision matters.

From the moral point of view, this liberty to make good our socio-economic system, or to debase it, has a value in its own right. For compulsory goodness ceases to be good. Although legislation in all industrial countries lays down what is in effect the minimum moral framework of social capitalism it is surely right that there should be plenty of sea-room, unmarked by buoys or navigation rules, where companies can work out their own policies and practices. Countries will differ as to how much self-regulation they preserve for business, both in theory and practice. But the risk of trusting industry and commerce to exercise self-discipline has proved fruitful, and cannot be abandoned if we would hold firm to our moral bearings. No freedom: no morality.

On the other hand, leaders in our developing social capitalist society will need a thorough appreciation of the planet-system of values by which they must conduct their free navigation.

The challenge to business leaders

Decisions at all levels in organizations now call most urgently for the exercise of the art of judgment. Why? Because decisions involve taking seriously their four disparate values – at times at tension if not at odds among each other in a concrete situation needing a decision. The challenge facing strategic-level leaders to make the *right* decision in the circumstances calls for a new form of integrity of the highest order.

For integrity is the hallmark of a person who is actively pursuing good ends which they value more than their own self-interest. Therefore it is a vital attribute for leaders in a social capitalist society already on the move towards a morally and socially better world.

An outstanding business leader, Sir Ernest Woodroofe, a former chairman of Unilever, highlighted the importance of integrity and judgment going hand-in-hand in an interview with Kenneth Harris for the *Observer*:

Harris: What single quality makes an industrial leader?
Woodroofe: No single quality, but an indispensable one is integrity. No doubt about it. Assuming certain qualities like efficiency, imagination, shrewdness, doggedness and so on, the all-essential one is integrity.
Harris: What do you mean by integrity in this context?

Woodroofe: Most decisions in business are based on uncertainties because you don't have all the information you would theoretically like to have, but having what you have, you must use your judgment and decide.

But, and this is what I mean by the overriding importance of integrity, the decision must be made within the framework of the responsibilities the businessman carries. He has responsibilities to the shareholders, the employees, the consumer, even the government of the day. He has to balance these responsibilities thoroughly, justly and without bias.

You could, for instance, make a decision which was to the benefit of your shareholders but to the detriment of the community as a whole. *Not* doing that, and knowing why you are not going to do it, and what not doing it is going to cost you, is what I mean by integrity.

Acting with integrity

Acting with integrity means that you are giving others grounds to trust you: you do not lie, cheat or deceive. Mistrust, once there, is like an axe to the tree of relationship. 'Trust, like the soul,' said the Roman author Catullus, 'once gone is gone forever.'

Integrity, in the sense of plain speaking and above-the-board dealing, is a key quality for all leaders. Shakespeare captured its essence in *Hamlet* (Act I, Scene III):

> *This above all: to thine own self be true,*
> *And it must follow, as the night to day,*
> *Thou canst not then be false to any man.*

Leaders who resort to cunning or crafty methods of manipulating people to their will may gain short-term advantages, but in the long run they forfeit trust. 'Subtlety may deceive you,' wrote Cromwell in a letter to Robert Barnard in January 1642. 'Integrity never will.' For integrity implies adherence to moral standards – especially truth and goodness – that lie outside oneself.

Integrity will always be tested, not least if money is involved. 'Few men have virtue to withstand the highest bidder,' observed George Washington. Yet if you permit someone to take away your honour, you permit them to remove a part of your soul. For integrity is the final inner keep of the mind, worth defending to the last when the outlying bastions and ramparts have fallen. Don't forget who you are, when you see what others can be like.

The primary meaning of integrity comes from its Latin ancestor *integer*, whole. By the middle of the sixteenth century, integrity had also acquired its moral sense: 'soundness of moral principle; the character of uncorrupted virtue; uprightness, honesty, sincerity'. Webster's Dictionary expanded this sense to embrace an adherence to a code of moral, artistic or other values.

Serving the truth, in the fuller sense as a value close to goodness and other than self, is central to the concept of integrity. It means accepting what is true, right or good from whatever quarter it comes. Here is an example of a man who did *not* have that attitude. Writing in *The Times*, a British civil servant added this footnote to the obituary of his erstwhile boss:

> Best of all was a remark of his to me which I have always treasured and tried to remember when I myself became a senior. I had mentioned, over tea, that I had just written a long minute to him, and said that I was not all sure that what I had said was right. 'My dear ….,' he replied, 'there is no such thing as right and wrong in our work. There is only your opinion and my opinion, and it so happens that, as I am the senior, mine will prevail.' What better *envoi* could any young man have on the threshold of a civil service career?

Fortunately, another contributor to the paper on that same day gave a possible answer to the last question. Recalling a conversation with Harry S. Truman when the latter came to Oxford University to receive an honorary degree, a professor recalled that the President told him he had another quotation on his desk, besides the well-known 'The buck stops here.' This was a sentence from the American writer and humourist Mark Twain: 'Always tell the truth; it will please some people and astonish the rest.'

A person of integrity, then, is honest to such a degree that they are incapable of being false to a trust, responsibility or pledge – or to their own standards of conduct. For integrity is the opposite of a condition where a person can be moved by opportunist or self-seeking impulses, which threaten to break up his or her unity as a whole being. It is a wholeness which stems from being true to truth. We know what it means when people say of a scholar or artist that he or she has integrity: they do not deceive themselves or other people, they are not manipulators.

Just why it is that people who have integrity in this sense create trust in others, I shall leave you to reflect upon at your leisure. Certainly, we all know that a person who deliberately misleads us by telling lies sooner or later forfeits our trust. It is a leadership principle which those political leaders of nations who lie to their people have been – and are – slow to learn, or have thought they will be able to get away with. But often they are found out in the long run, often greatly to their discomfort, for the truth has a way of surfacing into the light of day, however deeply it has been buried in the ground, at dead of night.

Lord Strang, head of the British Diplomatic Service during the Second World War, highlighted the nature and importance of judgment in his profession. 'The art of diplomacy resides,' he wrote in his biography, *Home and Abroad* (1951), 'in great measure, in the capacity to reach just judgments and to determine wise courses on incomplete information in conditions allowing too little time for reflection. Diplomats must have well-stored minds and they can with advantage be people of learning: but in essence, diplomacy is action, not study.'

Thus, Strang's first advice to new entrants to his profession is: 'Preserve a calm, clear judgment. The person who can keep their head and their temper will be at an advantage.'

He continued: 'Secondly, truthfulness. In spite of the current jibe, diplomatists, if they are any good, do not lie: if they did, they would lose the confidence of the governments to which they are accredited and be of no use to their own governments. All the best writers on the art of diplomacy emphasise this point.

'You will sometimes be sorely tempted to say less, or more, than the truth when making records of your conversations with foreign representatives, in order to show yourself to better advantage than the course of the conversation may have warranted. If you do much of this when you come to positions of authority, you will be found out in the end. Both sides will make a record of the talk and sooner or later both records may be published. Historians are quick to spot the inventor or prevaricator; you may be dead by then, but the reputation of your government and of your Service will suffer. This is a very insidious temptation.'

There is clearly a distinction to be made between being – for good reasons – economical with the truth and downright untruthful.

Confucius was insistent upon the importance of trustworthiness in a leader, and he recognized that in order to inspire others' trust, a leader must have integrity.

> The Master said, 'Duke Wen of Chin was crafty and lacked integrity. Duke Huan of Ch'i, on the other hand, had integrity and was not crafty.'

We can assume that Duke Wen was not acceptable to Confucius – how could he be? For integrity certainly implies, among other things, being trustworthy or reliable in word. It is not an exaggeration to say that Confucius regards integrity as the linchpin of moral character; indeed, he uses that very metaphor:

> The Master said, 'I do not see how a man can be acceptable who is untrustworthy in word. When a pin is missing in the yoke-bar of a large cart or in the collar-bar of a small cart, how can the cart be expected to go?'

'Integrity without knowledge is weak and useless, and knowledge without integrity is dangerous and dreadful,' Dr Samuel Johnson once said. Clearly, integrity on its own is never going to be enough: it is a foundation but not the actual house of the art of judgment.

* * * * * * *

George Washington (1732–99) was the first president of the United States and an example of moral uprightness to all his successors, some of whom have dropped the torch. In a letter to his close adviser James Madison, Washington writes,

> It is an old adage that honesty is the best policy. This applies to public as well as private life, to states as well as to individuals.

The presence of strong ambition in a person – I mean, ambition in the pejorative sense of an inordinate striving after rank and wealth – will usually test their integrity. For the promise of shortcuts to the top at the expense of one's moral values is sometimes just too tempting. Yet those who sacrifice their integrity upon the altar of ambition may well live to regret it bitterly. As a Chinese proverb expresses it, *He who sacrifices his integrity to achieve his ambition burns a picture to obtain the ashes.*

Humility

Humility is the clearness of soul that allows you to see reality – including the reality of oneself – as it really is.

Lord Beaverbrook (1879–1964), Canadian-born British Conservative politician and newspaper proprietor, who became minister for aircraft production in Churchill's wartime Cabinet, was clearly ambiguous about the value of humility. In his book, *Don't Trust to Luck* (1959), he tells us there are three great rules for the successful man who wishes to be happy: 'To do justly, and to love mercy, and to walk humbly... The quality of humility is by far the most difficult to attain. There is something deep down in the nature of a successful man of affairs which seems to conflict with it. His career is imbued with a sense of struggle and courage and conquest, and seems almost to invite *arrogance*.'

He adds: 'I cannot pretend to be humble myself. All I can confess is the knowledge that in so far as I could acquire humility I should be happier... Many instances prove that success and humility are not incompatible.'

Certainly, that is true of leaders of the first order when you study their lives. For example, Dwight D. Eisenhower discerned in Winston Churchill, whom he came to know well while planning for D-Day in 1944, that he exuded self-confidence, and to those who didn't know him well, he could come across as arrogant. But old friends, such as Lady Violet Bonham Carter, saw a different side to him. She once gently chided him for the persona he presented: 'You should remember, Winston, that you are just a worm like the rest of us.' 'Yes,' replied a beaming Churchill after a moment or two of thought, 'yes, I am a worm – but I am a *glow* worm.'

THE QUALITY OF HUMILITY

A SENSE OF HUMILITY IS a quality I have observed in every leader whom I have deeply admired. I have seen Winston Churchill with humble tears of gratitude on his cheeks as he thanked people for their help to Britain and the Allied cause.

My own conviction is that every leader should have enough humility to accept, publicly, the responsibility for the mistakes of the subordinates he has himself selected and, likewise, to give them credit, publicly, for their triumphs. I am aware that some popular theories of leadership hold that the top man must always keep his 'image' bright and shining. I believe, however, that in the long run fairness and honesty, and a generous attitude towards subordinates and associates, pay off.

DWIGHT D. EISENHOWER

A good strategic leader will certainly accept complete personal responsibility if the decision he or she has made leads to failure. They will not 'pass the buck' to their colleagues or subordinates. After the failure of his first attack on Quebec in 1775, General Wolfe wrote: 'The blame I take entirely upon my shoulders and I expect to suffer for it. Accidents cannot be helped. As much of the plan as was defective falls justly on me.'

Eisenhower also shouldered the responsibility of failure. The weather conditions in the first few days of June 1944 caused his air commander to argue for further postponement of the invasion of Europe. After consultation with his generals and specialist advisers, Eisenhower himself took the momentous decision to take the risk and go ahead on 6 June 1944. Before the invasion fleet set out, he wrote this press release, to be used if necessary:

> Our landings have failed and I have withdrawn the troops. My decision to attack at this time and place was based upon the best information available. The troops, the Air and the Navy did all that bravery and devotion to duty could do. If any blame or fault is attached to the attempt, it is mine alone.

Hitler exemplified the opposite side of the coin – irresponsibility. He persistently blamed the failure of his military plans upon the incompetence of his subordinates or their lack of will power, while taking for himself the credit of the early successes. When the Third Reich collapsed, Hitler castigated the German people for letting him down. He could neither see nor face his ultimate responsibility as leader.

To accept that one may have been wrong after a decision and to accept the consequences is only one aspect of humility. To be open to others and their ideas before a decision means that you do not believe you are a genius who alone knows what to do – this is an equally important facet of humility. As the Scottish proverb says: *The clan is greater than the chief.* A chief who believes this is more likely to consult the clan and listen to their ideas. As the writer G.K. Chesterton said, 'It is always the secure who are humble.'

'If you lack humility,' said James Blyth, a former chairman and chief executive of Boots in the 1990s, in a lecture on leadership, 'you are not a leader, not perhaps even a true person.' Blyth suggested that humility as a leader means confidence in that part of one's self that 'looks on tempests and is never shaken'. It is the ability to be closely in touch with the passing show, but not to get too embroiled in it.

Former Second Secretary-General of the United Nations Dag Hammarskjöld is perhaps the leader in modern times who has reflected most deeply on the meaning of humility. In Hammarskjöld's private journal, humility is a central theme. Later published posthumously in Swedish with the title of *Väg*

Märken ('Way Marks') – such as the stone cairns that guide the fell walker on snowbound or mist-shrouded paths – and in English as *Markings*, the journal contains, for example, his observation on humility:

29.7.59

Humility is just as much the opposite of self-abasement as it is of self-exaltation. To be humble *is not to make comparisons*. Secure in its reality, the self is neither better nor worse, bigger nor smaller, than anything else in the universe. It *is* – is nothing, yet at the same time one with everything. It is in this sense that humility is absolute self-effacement.

The great Japanese potter Shoji Hamada (1894–1978) referred to humility as 'losing one's tail' – the tail being an excessive egoism. Incidentally, there is a fine distinction in the English language between *egoism* and *egotism*. *Egoism* emphasizes a concentration on oneself, one's interests and one's needs; it commonly implies self-interest, especially as opposed to altruism or interest in others, as the inner spring of one's acts or as the measure by which all things we judge.

Egotism stresses the tendency to attract attention to and centre interest on oneself, one's thoughts or one's achievements. It is a trait difficult to disguise as it is manifest in the practice of continually talking about oneself, usually with an excessive use of 'I' and 'me'.

A SHORT COURSE ON LEADERSHIP

The six most important words: 'I admit I made a mistake.'
The five most important words: 'I am proud of you.'
The four most important words: 'What is your opinion?'
The three most important words: 'If you please.'
The two most important words: 'Thank you.'
The one most important word: 'We.'
And the least important word: 'I.'

The leadership that Eisenhower displayed as the Supreme Commander in Europe in the closing years of the Second World War reflected these values of integrity and humility, vital ingredients in the art of judgment. In the words of Cambridge University's Public Orator when an honorary degree was conferred upon Eisenhower: 'He showed himself such an example of kindly wisdom, such a combination of serious purpose, humanity, and courtesy, that the others soon had no thought in their minds save to labour with one common will for the success of all.'

Intellectual humility

All these aspects of humility go into the making of a good leader and a leader for good. No wonder it has come to be valued so highly. Yet why is humility an *intellectual* virtue, as I have suggested it is? What part does it play in the art of judgment?

The simple answer is that intellectual humility is knowing what you know and being clear about what you do not know. Strangely enough, that gives you an advantage that not all people enjoy. For, as Mark Twain said: 'It ain't what you don't know that gets you into trouble. It's what you know for sure that just ain't so.'

Consider this story about Socrates, which we owe to his most famous student, Plato:

THE SECRET OF SOCRATES

I WENT TO INTERVIEW A man with a high reputation for wisdom, because I felt that here if anywhere I should succeed in disproving the oracle and pointing out to my divine authority 'You said that I was the wisest of men, but here is a man who is wiser than I am.'

Well, I gave a thorough examination to this person, and in conversation with him I formed the impression that although in many people's opinion, and especially in his own, he appeared to be wise, in fact he was not. Then when I began to try to show him that he only thought he was wise and was not really so, my efforts were resented both by him and by many of the other people present.

However, I reflected as I walked away: 'Well, I am certainly wiser than this man. It is only too likely that neither of us has any knowledge to boast of; but he thinks that he knows something which he does not know, whereas I am quite conscious of my ignorance. At any rate it seems that I am wiser than he is to this small extent, that I do not think that I know what I do not know...

As I pursued my investigation, my honest impression was that the people with the greatest reputations were almost entirely deficient, while others who were supposed to be their inferiors were much better qualified in practical intelligence.

Sir William Osler (1849–1919), often referred to as the 'father of modern medicine', not only exemplified the qualities of a good doctor but also taught them to generations of medical students in his native Canada and at Oxford University in the United Kingdom. Among those qualities he afforded Socratic intellectual humility a place of honour. 'In these days,' he wrote, 'of aggressive self-assertion, when the stress of competition is so keen and the desire to make the most of oneself so universal, it may seem a little old-fashioned to preach the necessity of this virtue, but I insist for its own sake, and for the sake of what it brings, that a due humility should take the place on the list.'

> *Errors of judgment must occur in the practice of an art which consists largely of balancing probabilities.*
>
> SIR WILLIAM OSLER

Key points: The role of values

- 'We navigate by the same stars,' Winston Churchill once said of President De Gaulle. Values are like stars: we steer by them; they inform all our judgments. The greatest of them all is the leading star – truth;

- In our new global *social capitalist* environment, guidance at the highest level comes from a pattern or constellation of four stars: *Money*, *Society*, the *Individual* and *Nature*. A good business leader of today and tomorrow is one who balances these values in all their judgments with complete integrity;

- According to an ancient Roman proverb, *integrity is the noblest possession*. Integrity implies trustworthiness and incorruptibility to a degree that one is incapable of being false to a trust;

- Humility is the quality that keeps you always open to learn more. It is the necessary condition for excellence in leadership;

- Intellectual humility is a real awareness of where the dividing line falls between your knowledge and your ignorance, and indeed between *our* knowledge and *our* ignorance. Which do you think is the greater?

- The value you add comes from the values you hold.

In our complex and interdependent world, vulnerable to disruption, few things are more important than the quality and credibility of leaders.

10

Practical wisdom

*Good sense, disciplined by experience and inspired by
goodness, issues in practical wisdom.*

SAMUEL SMILES

WISDOM OUTRANKS ALL the other words in its neighbour-
hood – discernment, discrimination, judgment, sagacity, sense –
when it comes to denoting mental qualities that have to do with
the ability to understand situations, anticipate consequences and
make sound decisions.

For wisdom (in Greek *sophia*) suggests a rare combination
of discretion, maturity, keenness of intellect, broad experience,
extensive learning, profound thought and compassionate
understanding. In its wider application wisdom implies the
highest and noblest exercise of the faculties of moral nature as
well as of the intellect.

In relation to practical affairs, the Ancient Greeks had a different word for it – *phronesis*. The Romans translated it as *prudentia*, and it eventually found its way into English as *prudence*. But that doesn't do it justice; the full meaning of *phronesis* is *practical wisdom*. It is actually the nearest word to judgment in the sense that I have been describing and exploring it in these pages in the classical languages of Greek and Latin.

In Aristotle's discussion of ethics, *phronesis* plays a leading role, which has helped to preserve the concept to this day. It is essentially the practical judgment as to what to do and how to do it in a morally challenging situation. According to Aristotle, *phronesis* is 'imperative' – it gives orders.

A *phroninos* (a practically wise person) is always a doer, but one who acts with skill and judgment. In the Greek New Testament gospels, for example, it is the wise man (*phroninos*) who builds his house on rock, whereas his foolish neighbour knows no better than to build his house on sand. Therefore, when the winter storms come, one house predictably stands and the other one predictably falls.

In Aristotle's writings, however, the practically wise person is far more than just an experienced builder. Practical wisdom is the faculty that enables us to discover what is good for the community at large. At the global level in our own era that means identifying what makes for the good as a whole for mankind, both present and to come, for all life on our complex and fragile planet.

Incidentally, goodness of this kind is something we discern in a person's *character*, not primarily in their *personality*. Character, derived from the name of the Greek tool used for engraving on stone or metal, commonly indicates all the attributes or features which mark out one as an individual. But in this context, however, it applies more specifically to the aggregate of *moral* qualities by which a person is judged, apart that is from such factors as their intelligence, competence, experience or special talents.

Why does *goodness* enter into the sphere of judgment? Because many of the decisions which you will face as a leader will have a moral dimension to them. If you lack practical wisdom – *intelligence, experience and goodness* – your judgment may be deficient in that vital strand of goodness when it comes to moral judgment. The morally colour blind are among the most dangerous of our fellow citizens.

Not to know right from wrong as a leader is worse than not knowing port from starboard. A ship with such a morally blind leader at the helm is bound to crash into the rocks. According to an old Hebrew proverb, *When God wants to punish his people he sends them a blind shepherd*.

For the Ancient Greeks, practical wisdom is the crown of qualities they looked for in leaders. An agile mind, a good eye and immediate understanding of any new situation... these are some of the elements that go to making practical wisdom. Add to that political clear-sightedness. Themistocles, the man whom his contemporaries nicknamed Odysseus by reason of his *phronesis* or practical wisdom, personified these qualities. Born of a father of no particular distinction and an alien mother, as a boy he showed unusual ability and application. Indeed, his career proved a point made by Pericles, that in Athens 'what counts is not membership of a particular class, but the actual ability which the man possesses'.

As Thucydides wrote in his history of the war between Athens and Sparta, few surpassed Themistocles in practical wisdom:

Themistocles was a man who showed an unmistakable natural genius; in this respect he was quite exceptional, and beyond all others deserved our admiration. Without studying a subject in advance or deliberating over it later, but using simply the intelligence that was his by nature, he had the power to reach the right conclusion in matters that have to be settled on the spur of the moment and do not admit of long discussions, and in estimating what was likely to happen, his forecasts of the future were always more reliable than those of others.

He could perfectly well explain any subject with which he was familiar, and even outside his own department he was still capable of giving an excellent opinion. He was particularly remarkable at looking into the future and seeing there the hidden possibilities for good or evil. To sum him up in a few words, it may be said that through force of genius and by rapidity of action this man was supreme at doing precisely the right thing at precisely the right moment.

Experience does tend to breed confidence in one's own judgment. Admiral Horatio Nelson (1758–1805), for example, could declare – with some justification: 'When I follow my own head, I am, in general, much more correct in my judgment than following the opinion of others.' Yet there is always the danger of overconfidence. The chief symptoms are a loss of humble open-mindedness, a growing indifference to the opinions of others well qualified to give their views and advice, a refusal – eventually – to even listen to others.

Time is a limited resource for all of us. Leaders at the senior level have to be able to discriminate between those around them – or approaching them – who have something relevant and important to say, and can say it concisely, and those who lack these two credentials. This principle applies to discussion with groups as well as with individuals.

As Onasander, the Greek author of a short but comprehensive work on the role of a general, entitled *Strategikos* and written in the first century CE, implies, there is a golden mean to be found between confidence in your own judgment and being open to the judgments of others, as voiced either collectively or individually:

> The general must be neither so unstable in his judgment that he entirely mistrusts himself, nor so obstinate as to think that nothing that another person has thought up is going to be better than what he himself thinks. Inevitably if a leader heeds everyone else and never himself, he will suffer numerous reverses. On the other hand, if he virtually never listens to others but always only to himself, he will also make many mistakes in consequence.

At the end of the day, however, especially in such personal matters as career or family choices, you do have to follow your own judgment. The best advice is *Listen–Think–Act*. As Montaigne puts it in a nutshell: 'I listen with attention to the judgments of all men; but as far as I can remember, I have followed none but my own.'

'Any leader worth his salt,' Eisenhower adds, 'must of course possess a certain amount of ego, a justifiable pride in his own accomplishments. But if he is a truly great leader, the cause must predominate over self.' An old and respected commander of mine used to say, 'Always take your job seriously, never yourself.' That advice underlines the importance of a leader, especially at the most senior levels: retaining their sense of humour, for humour keeps things in proportion, it is the antidote to any form of self-importance. If you feel that humility is beyond your reach, make sure that you hang onto a sense of humour!

We find that very same principle – job first, self second – expressed by one of the great political orators of the nineteenth century, William Ewart Gladstone (1809–98), Prime Minister of England:

We are to respect our responsibilities, not ourselves.

We are to respect the duties of which we are capable, not our capabilities simply considered.

There is to be no complacent self-contemplation, ruminating on self.

When the self is viewed, it must always be in the most intimate connexion with its purpose.

> *Sense shines with double lustre when it is set in humility. An able yet humble man is a jewel worth a kingdom.*
>
> WILLIAM PENN

Key points: Practical wisdom

- Practical wisdom is an alchemist's mixture of *intelligence, experience and goodness*. It is the exercise of judgment on the highest level known to us;

- As such, it serves us as a kind of guiding ideal: something that we can keep before us and aspire to while knowing that we shall never reach it. It is another star for your journey on what Shakespeare called 'life's uncertain voyage';

- Failure is instructive. The person who really thinks learns quite as much from their failures as from their successes – that's providing they reflect upon them in the cool hour, and extract their lessons;

- The Israeli diplomat and writer Abba Eban (1915–2002) once said, 'People and nations behave wisely – once they have exhausted all other alternatives.' Practical wisdom alone can release us – and you – from that particular tyranny;

- Strategic leadership differs not in kind but in magnitude of issues and scale of complexity encountered. It calls for a commensurate level of what the Greeks called *phronesis*, practical wisdom;

- 'A leader is not so much clever,' said Henry Kissinger, 'as lucid and clear-sighted.' Clear thinking is your path to practical wisdom. By the way, don't forget to take your sense of humour with you!

You are not born a leader, you become one.
PROVERB OF THE BAMBILEKE PEOPLE IN WEST AFRICA

Conclusion

AMID THE CARNAGE of the Greek tragedy *Antigone* written by Sophocles around 442 BCE, portraying a mighty king brought low by his own misrule, a messenger offers an insight to redeem all the suffering: 'Of all the ills afflicting men,' he observes, 'the worst is lack of judgment.'

Exercising good judgment – be it in your professional or personal life – is among the more difficult tasks for human beings and also among the most needful. Yet there are some simple steps that we can all take to progress in the art of judgment, even though none of us will ever attain mastery of it.

The first step yields half of all the benefits of this book: it is to become a lover of truth. The Scottish nineteenth-century author and scientist Henry Drummond (1851–97), famous for his address on 1 Corinthians 13 entitled *The Greatest Thing in the World*, gives us a thumbnail sketch of what it means to a person:

> He will accept only what is real; he will strive to get at facts; he will search for Truth with a humble and unbiased mind, and cherish whatever he finds at any sacrifice.

According to the novelist and poet A.E. Housman (1859–1936), 'The faintest of all human passions is the love of Truth.' Yes, but our faintest passions are often the highest.

What Tolstoy taught me is just what practical value the truth has for us – again, personally and in professional decision-making. Hear him again:

> *Seek the truth: it always shows us*
> *What we should do,*
> *What we should not do,*
> *And what we should stop doing.*

With such a lantern for our feet, we may get bewildered or lost for a time but the mist will lift and we shall find the path again.

Trust in your own judgment – however tentatively at first – and exercise it whenever you have need or opportunity to do so. Experience then corrects you and becomes your best teacher. For, as Scottish author and government reformer Samuel Smiles (1812–1904) observed:

> Practical wisdom is only to be learned in the school of experience. Precepts and instructions are useful so far as they go, but, without the discipline of real life, they remain of the nature of theory only.

True, yet practically wise people *know* that they need to – and enjoy – listening and learning from others. For the School of

Experience – if you *only* rely on that – may charge very high fees, and you may find that you are too old to apply what you have learnt the hard way. Hence my advice to you can be summed up as 'learn from others but always exercise your own judgment'. As the Chinese proverb says:

> *Listen to all, pluck a feather from every passing goose, but follow no one absolutely.*

INDEX